KV-051-819

Penal Policy
and
Political Culture
in England and Wales

FOUR ESSAYS ON POLICY AND PROCESS

Mick Ryan

WATERSIDE PRESS
WINCHESTER

Penal Policy and Political Culture
in England and Wales

CONTENTS

Preface

It must be something like 20 years ago that I began negotiating with Professor Bernard Crick and Professor Patrick Seyd about the framework for a book which was later published as *The Politics of Penal Reform* (1983) in the Fontana/Longman series, *Politics Today*.

In the intervening years it has often been suggested to me that I update this text. I have previously resisted this for two reasons. The first is that there is little added value in keeping the same framework, and then simply inserting new data, even when there is plenty of data to add, as there was in this case. Second, although the original framework worked well enough, I later concluded, for a number of reasons, it was not the best framework to have adopted.

There the matter rested until fairly recently when several of my students argued that an updated *The Politics of Penal Reform* was surely justified, if for no other reason than to highlight the very significant changes that had taken place in penal policy and the penal policy making process between the New Right of the 1980s and New Labour of the 1990s, not least around the idea of the public voice(s), the subject of my most recent writing.

I was eventually convinced by this argument, but in order to do something new, and I trust, better, I have employed a totally different framework which is encapsulated in four long essays. These both link and contrast the period since 1945 with the present day.

The first essay takes us from the 1940s into the first part of the 1960s. These were the days when the men from the Ministry and their small coterie of advisors knew best. The second looks at the counter culture of the 1960s into the 1970s when official voices were challenged from below. The third and fourth essays cover the period of the New Right and New Labour. The essays can be read separately, though ideally they should be considered together and sequentially to reveal both the continuities and discontinuities of penal policy and penal policy making in England and Wales.

I would not go as far as to say that the framework I have used can be described as a heuristic one, with the all-embracing explanatory potential this suggests, but I trust it is at least a suggestive framework which will shed some light on how British penal policy, and the penal policy making process, have been shaped since 1945 by other, wider changes in British political culture.

It goes without saying that others will chronicle penal change in this period using different frameworks. Each framework will have a certain validity; it is up to the reader to decide which he or she finds the most illuminating, not least for the purposes they have in mind. I put it like this because there are no innocent readers, any more than there are innocent writers or reviewers.

I have tried to write as clearly as possible, not only for undergraduates and criminal justice professionals, but also for interested members of the public. I have always understood Professor Bernard Crick's emphasis on political education to go beyond teaching "citizenship" to sixth formers, to place on academics an obligation to communicate beyond the academy on issues that are politically important. In pursuit of this goal I have mostly eschewed detailed footnotes, giving PRO references, for example, in the main text. I trust that my more routine references are reasonably full.

Mick Ryan June 2002

Acknowledgements

Given the nature of this exercise, I have drawn on a lot of my own published research. However, employing a new framework inevitably threw up new questions, revealed new gaps and called for fresh research.

In this context I would like to thank two former Greenwich University students, Dr Andy Wilson and Dr Don Prichard. The latter was one of my own PhD students who directed me, *en passant* so to speak, to material on the old Prison Commission and checked many other references, while the former was employed under my direction in 1999 to research a number of areas, but particularly material for my first and third essays. I am grateful to the Research Board for the Business, Social Science and Humanities Schools at the University of Greenwich for funding his work.

Another Greenwich post graduate research student, Anne Logan, has also helped. Her ongoing work in uncovering the contribution made by women magistrates to both the substance and administration of criminal justice policy generally will help to refine, to a degree, the male, metropolitan bias in penal affairs that I identify.

I would also like to thank Stephen Nathan of the Prison Reform Trust whose endeavours helped bring me up to speed on prison privatization which I discuss in *Part III*. Since I left this behind me as a particular research interest in the early 1990s, much more has come to light about how the private sector secured this significant change in the way penal services are delivered. Business was even better connected to the Conservative Party than I had surmised.

Keith Rogers at the Home Office's Research Development and Statistics Directorate also deserves my thanks. He provided me with the broad brush prison population statistics for the years 1978 and 1998 to which I refer in my fourth essay.

I should also like to thank Professor Mike Hough at South Bank University. We have been preoccupied, in our different ways, with researching and writing about the public voice(s) in recent years, and I was therefore especially grateful to be invited to look through the relevant parts of *Penal Populism and Public Opinion* (Oxford University Press, 2002). References to this in my fourth essay come from *Chapter 5* of the manuscript text.

Important for the first essay was Dr Mike Nellis now at the University of Birmingham. We first met when he was a young probation officer in Greenwich and we were members of RAP's governing Nucleus in East London. Although our paths have not crossed that much since then, I have taken the opportunity to remind him that it was his suggestion that RAP call its journal *The Abolitionist*. But more to the present point, I remembered that he has a copious knowledge of British prison writing, and it was the references he generously supplied that helped provide me with the prisoners' point of view for the 1950s.

Another person who was perhaps more valuable than he, or I, realized at the time when he agreed to be interviewed in Oxford in the summer of 2000 was former civil servant David Faulkner. At first I thought that he had revealed very little, but on reflection I came to realize that he had told me a good deal about the politics of the Criminal Justice Act 1991 and the role (and mood) of the higher civil service in government in the 1980s and early 1990s. I have indicated in the text where I have drawn on this interview.

Given the nature of my academic background and the interpretation I put forward, it is also appropriate to mention several political scientists. Dr Brian Neve, University of Bath, Dr Geraint Williams, University of Sheffield and Dr David Woodhead, University of Greenwich, who both pointed me towards interesting materials relevant to the issue of populism which I interrogate in my last essay. Dr Alan Foster and Paul Wingrove at the University of Greenwich were also unfailingly helpful.

Three close academic colleagues agreed to go through my text, Professor Joe Sim, Dr Tony Ward and Professor Vincenzo Ruggiero. I first came across Joe Sim when he came to talk to a RAP conference about the legal battle he and Mike Fitzgerald had waged with the Home Office over some "controversial" material in the first print run of *British Prisons* (Oxford, 1979). This struggle serves as a very good example of how the Home Office then used the threat of legal action in an attempt to stifle criticism. I was struck by Joe Sim's determination to see this battle through, to tell the truth about the state of our prisons in the 1970s. He retains that determination and integrity still, and while we do not always agree, I invariably value and learn from what he has to say.

I have known Tony Ward since we appointed him at RAP in 1980. He later edited *The Abolitionist* and was made one of two joint organizers of INQUEST which had been set up to investigate deaths in State custody following the death of Blair Peach in 1979. Since then we have researched and written a good deal together and sometimes it is genuinely difficult, looking back, to remember who had this or that idea. However, we have never been afraid to disagree, so I am grateful that he took the time to look over the manuscript, and it is not the first time I have bothered him.

Vincenzo Ruggiero came to London from Italy in the late 1980s as a self-imposed political exile after a history in *Lotta Continua* and working to promote prison writing. When we talked after hours at INQUEST he always stressed the need to understand penal systems in their very specific, dynamic national cultures. I have not forgotten these conversations, as I trust these four essays will demonstrate.

If I have bothered all these colleagues, then I have, of course, bothered Joan Ryan a good deal more! It is therefore appropriate for me to warmly thank her, for the intellectual support she has given me not only during this particular project, but also during many other academic projects stretching back over many years. I would have achieved far less without her, that is certain.

David Evans in the Dreadnaught Library at the University of Greenwich was unfailingly helpful and courteous, as were the administrative staff in the School of Humanities.

Finally, I must thank my publisher, Bryan Gibson. He was more than willing to take on board what was obviously going to be a very political text, aspects of which he was likely to disagree with. Furthermore, he has been very patient as my department first went through an audit, and was moved "lock, stock and barrel" to the Old Royal Naval College at Greenwich. I trust that others will keep to their timetables rather better than I was able to do, given my teaching commitments at Greenwich.

Mick Ryan June 2002

Abbreviations

ACOP	Association of the Chief Officers of Probation[1]
ACPO	Association of Chief Police Officers
ACPS	Advisory Council on the Penal System
ACTO	Advisory Council on the Treatment of Offenders
ASI	Adam Smith Institute
BMA	British Medical Association
CBI	Confederation of British Industry
CCA	Corrections Corporation of America
CND	Campaign for Nuclear Disarmament
GLC	Greater London Council[2]
Howard League	Howard League for Penal Reform
KPI	Key performance indicator
MUFTI	Minimal use of force tactical intervention
NACRO	National Association for the Care and Resettlement of Offenders
NAPO	National Association of Probation Officers
NAVSS	National Association of Victims Support Schemes
NCCL	National Council for Civil Liberties
NDC	National Deviancy Conference
NMAG	NAPO Members Action Group
NPM	New public management
NSPCC	National Society for the Prevention of Cruelty to Children
PFI	Private Finance Initiative
PMS	Prison Medical Service
POA	Prison Officers' Association
PPP	Private public partnerships
PRO	Public Record Office
PROP	Preservation of the Rights of Prisoners
PRT	Prison Reform Trust
RAP	Radical Alternatives to Prison
SNOP	Statement of National Objectives
TUC	Trades Union Congress
TUPE	European Business Transfer Directive
UKDS	United Kingdom Detention Services
VFM	Value for money (audit)
WIP	Women in Prison
YOI	Young offender institution

---

[1] Now defunct. Chief probation officers belong to the Association of Probation Boards.

[2] The GLC was abolished in the mid-1980s.

PART I

Elites

In this first essay I want to argue that the Welfare Consensus that existed in Britain after 1945, and which arguably lasted well into the 1960s, was slow to get started in respect of penal change; that the support that it generated between the political parties to provide for the poor, the sick and the unemployed was not that easily translated into support for a more tolerant penal system, not least among members of the wider public.

However, the tension that this suggests was masked to a degree because the making of penal policy at this time in England and Wales was partly shielded from the public by a small metropolitan elite which used both the formal and informal processes of a highly centralized State apparatus to make the main lines of penal policy, and oversee its administration, away from the public gaze, and away from public or media interference.

This should not suggest that there was no public or media criticism of these generally more liberal policies, though I will suggest that they were not all that liberal, nor that the metropolitan elite which I identify was always united. On the contrary, it split into factions from time to time over tactics, with some factions in the Lords and among the judiciary in alliance with—though not always—the wider public whose opinions on penal policy were mostly more negotiated than accommodated.

Negotiating public opposition was therefore necessary, and the role of the higher Civil Service in managing this was central, though again, it was not without its constraints.

My contention is that this top down, closed—clubbable almost—way of doing business was the result of wider political and cultural forces which had little to do with the penal system per se, and which were only later to be disturbed by wider social, intellectual and cultural changes which took shape in the middle to late 1960s, and which will be the subject of my second essay.

THE POSTWAR WELFARE CONSENSUS AND PENAL CHANGE

When the Labour Party swept to power in 1945 it began the economic and social reconstruction of a country exhausted by war. Central to this reconstruction was a large scale programme of nationalization. The mines, steel and transport were all nationalized, while docks and harbours also came into public ownership as did the basic utilities: gas, electricity and water. The Bank of England was also placed firmly under government control as Labour sought to manage the economy, not only regulating internal demand according to Keynesian principles to secure full employment, but also acknowledging the responsibilities of the international monetary settlement secured at Bretton Woods in 1944.[1]

In addition to taking over what were described as the "commanding heights" of the economy, Labour began the long process of consolidating the Welfare State, most notably through the introduction of the National Health Service and carrying through the expansion of universal secondary education envisaged by the Education Act 1944. All these measures were thought necessary for an assault on what Beveridge (HMSO 1942) had identified as the five great giants: want, squalor, idleness, disease and ignorance.

In this new world where the individual was to be cared for from the "cradle to the grave" the extent and reach of government was inevitably increased; it could hardly be otherwise where the State rather than the market was being called upon to deliver the new Jerusalem. This meant an inevitable rise in the number of civil servants. By 1950 there were over 684,000 non-industrial civil servants (and rising) compared with only 387,400 in 1939 (Mackenzie and Grove 1957). Big government, top down, unitary government, was good government.

True, some of these changes—including the growth of the central State apparatus—met with spirited resistance in Parliament at the time, but in the event only a few were overturned when the Conservatives came back into government in 1951, nor was any serious attempt made to re-invigorate local government. Indeed, during their 13 years in office between 1951 and 1964 Conservative governments sought more *corporate* approaches to managing the economy from the centre in alliance with the Confederation of British Industry (CBI) and the Trades Union Congress (TUC) and significantly increased expenditure on the Welfare State.

Fears that the British model of government might one day translate into the bureaucratic centralism that had come to characterize the inert eastern bloc were few, and in the immediate postwar decades Hayek's *The Road to Serfdom* (1944) was a voice in the wilderness. Even Churchill's promise of a "bonfire of controls" had not been accompanied by the rhetoric of the "nanny State" or government "overload" which began to be heard in the 1970s.

It has been argued that the nature and scope of the Welfare Consensus had implications for penal policy, giving it a less repressive edge. Leon Radzinowicz, who advised successive postwar governments has observed:

---

[1] For details of this settlement, see Pollard S. (1992), *The Development of the British Economy 1914–1990*, London: Edward Arnold.

The continued advancement of social policy, in the widest sense of the term, was increasingly being recognized as one of the more vital and sensitive tasks of the state. This evolution inevitably exercised a profound influence on the evolution of criminal policy. A state which recognizes, as one of the basic aims of its domestic policy, improvements in the condition of the population especially of its poor and underprivileged strata of society, cannot maintain a merely, formal passive attitude towards penal repression ... Under such a political climate social policy and criminal policy come closer to each other ... at certain sensitive crossings.

(Radzinowicz 1999, p 115)

Official discourse and practice at the time lend some support to this argument, I would acknowledge, and it is certainly an attractive, progressive interpretation of postwar criminal justice policy: it carries with it an implicit recognition that many of those who were subject to penal sanctions had themselves been subject to one, or more often, a combination of the great giants identified by Beveridge. What offenders needed, therefore, was welfare support rather than punishment, and as the conditions which applied to the very poorest were upgraded, so too should theirs be. However, Radzinowicz's argument requires both amplification and qualification.

In the first place, so baldly stated it fails to make clear that the Welfare Consensus itself represents the historic postwar compromise between capital and labour: the direct consequence, not of some beneficent high minded State, but of a prolonged struggle by working class people who had at last, through the Labour Party, secured a workable majority in Parliament (having previously only briefly held office as minority governments in the 1920s). So, the gains in welfare provision which may have helped to soften the tone around the treatment of offenders and ex-offenders were arguably hard won as part of a wider social democratic settlement about limiting the destructive power of an unfettered market.

Second, the immediate postwar Labour government was too concerned with managing the economy and forcing through its changes to the health and education services to radically overhaul its criminal justice policy, and penal policy in particular. As a consequence the Criminal Justice Act 1948 was hardly innovative. Indeed, it was simply a revised version of the Criminal Justice Bill (1938) which had previously been shelved because of the outbreak of war with Germany. Furthermore, while this Act abolished the use of corporal punishment as a sentence of the courts, it also introduced detention centres to give young offenders a "short, sharp shock" and lowered the age at which more serious young offenders might be sent to Borstal. A new sentence, corrective training, was also introduced for petty persistent adult offenders, and the maximum period for preventive detention was raised from ten to 14 years. These were far from progressive measures, signalling more a *continuity* in penal strategies than any abrupt change. So, while the 1948 Act may not quite have merited the label "penological dinosaur" (Morris 1989), it hardly heralded the more progressive, welfare directed approach that Radzinowicz seeks to identify (and to be associated with).

Finally, apart from having more important priorities, the truth of the matter appears to be that while the public—Labour supporters included—

acknowledged that the five great giants which the newly created Welfare State was to eradicate played their part in explaining crime, there is no evidence that most people were entirely convinced that offenders were simply—or even mostly—the hapless victims of their environment. Putting the welfare of such offenders first was, therefore, not always uppermost in the public's minds. The poor and the sick were judged far more deserving, and connecting welfare to punishment was a link that frequently had to be fought for, defended and re-made by liberal progressives to a sceptical public, sometimes even against senior members of the judiciary who actively worked to undo that link.

Conflicts over the postwar abolition of corporal and capital punishment well illustrate this tension. The abolition of corporal punishment in the Criminal Justice Act 1948 referred to above—it was not abolished in prisons by the way, but only as a sentence of the court—was vigorously resisted in the House of Lords. It was claimed, and with some justification, that abolition was opposed by the public and some members of the police and prison services as well as the judiciary. However, although the government eventually got this measure through Parliament, its intentions were to a degree undermined by some judges who found other ways of inflicting, as they saw it, commensurate pain. When sentencing two young men for an assault in 1950 Lord Chief Justice Goddard made no bones about what he was up to:

> The sentence I am about to pass on you may be a warning to others of a like kidney. It is not for me to criticize the wisdom of Parliament that prevents me from doing what I might have done 18 months ago when I could have had you whipped and given you a short sentence. I am going to pass a long sentence as I am satisfied that there is no other way of dealing with it. It is not a case for Borstal ... (*The Times*, 1 March 1950)

We can presume that Goddard had been less scornful of the "wisdom of Parliament" when it rejected the abolition of capital punishment, tabled as an amendment to the same Act, after their Lordships had strenuously opposed this in terms more reminiscent of the Parliamentary struggle to reform the notorious Bloody Code in the eighteenth century than the rhetoric of welfare. Lord Goddard and his supporters were hard men. Penal discipline was a dark business, its terror an instrument to secure order among the lower classes.

To make these several qualifications is not to deny the postwar Welfare Consensus, nor to suggest that it did not have some generally progressive impact on penal practice. But it is to suggest that welfare and punishment, which always tend to coexist in modern penal systems as mechanisms to regulate and control (Garland 1985; Garland 1990), were together in the immediate postwar period in a far more even measure than is suggested by commentators such as Radzinowicz who understandably like to claim the moral high ground. So the welfare thrust of postwar penal policy was reluctantly conceded and did not run deep.

Furthermore, the examples of corporal and capital punishment well illustrate one of my principal themes, namely, that cross-class and cross-professional alliances were forged around penal issues at this time. This suggests a degree of conflict between the metropolitan elite who made penal policy, those who administered it, and the wider stakeholders in the criminal justice process: the public. I shall return to these examples later.

In the meantime, however, and in order to explore and understand these tensions, I want to begin by looking at the machinery of government in this period. My contention here is that in the decades immediately following 1945—indeed until well into the 1970s—penal policy making was in the hands of a relatively small, male metropolitan elite which, although never wholly in agreement, nonetheless saw itself as a barrier against what it took to be a more punitive public mostly more interested in punishment than in welfare or reform (as indeed were many judges and magistrates).

THE ROLE OF THE HOME OFFICE AND SENIOR CIVIL SERVANTS

The Home Office was well suited to accommodate the postwar growth in central government administration. The reasons for this are mainly historical.

One of the concomitants of industrialization in Britain was State control over the criminal justice system. The State rather than private citizens became responsible for prosecuting those who broke the criminal law and for managing the courts, while through a series of amalgamations and regulations the police who enforced the law slowly came under central government direction. As for the penal system itself, prisons were comprehensively nationalized overnight in 1877 and every detail of prisoners' lives, from their diet to their daily work routines, was laid down at the centre, as were prison officers' conditions of service. By the early part of the twentieth century industrial and reform schools had also been brought under government inspection and a Children's Branch at the Home Office established.

Local initiative and practice could still be found in parts of the criminal justice system, it is true. Probation officers, for instance, continued to be appointed by magistrates' committees and worked to local courts. Furthermore, the Victorian administrative instrument, the Prison Commission, continued to exist until it was incorporated into the Home Office in 1963. The independence of the Commission from the Home Office at this time, however, is easy to exaggerate (Lewis 1997; HMSO 1979, vol. 1). While the Commission had originally enjoyed a good deal of autonomy, under the direction firstly of Jebb and subsequently of Du Cane, both Royal Engineers seen as experts in managing large numbers of people, by the late nineteenth century it had become a desirable posting for senior First Division generalist civil servants. This inevitably led to "close cooperation with central government officials in the formation of penal policy", as Roy Macleod has reminded us (1988, p 70). This process accelerated after 1963 (HMSO 1979, vol. 1).

To illustrate this closeness it is instructive that much of the original thinking behind the 1938 Criminal Justice Bill was attributable to Sir Alexander Maxwell, an Oxford educated prison commissioner, who in the late 1930s became the Permanent Secretary at the Home Office under Samuel Hoare (Templewood 1954). Permanent Secretaries' contact with the prison system, their overview of the criminal justice system as a whole, and their grasp of the increasingly complex administrative apparatus which was the Home Office, inevitably gave them great power and influence. For example, it is widely accepted that one of

Maxwell's successors, Sir Frank Newsom, persuaded Labour's first postwar Home Secretary Chuter Ede to oppose the abolition of capital punishment, even though abolition was official Labour Party policy (Christoph 1962). So powerful were these officials that the secretary of the Howard League for Penal Reform thought it was highly unusual—a testimony to R A Butler's political status—for the new Home Secretary to have met him at the Home Office in the 1950s, privately, without the presence of his Permanent Secretary.

The thinly disguised power of these Whitehall mandarins with their insular attitudes came to be criticized in the 1960s. Moreover, it seems to have been generally accepted that the Home Office was more insular and hierarchical than most departments. Many of its senior officials had spent only a short time outside the Home Office during their long careers. Roy Jenkins, a reforming Labour Home Secretary in the 1960s, for example, recalled that compared with the Treasury where debates and disagreements were commonplace, in the Home Office: "Everything, eventually came through one single source, distilled in the initials of the Permanent Secretary" (Jenkins 1975, p 211).

Jenkins recalls how on one occasion he almost reduced his Permanent Secretary to tears. This was not so much because Jenkins was challenging a revered Home Office policy, but more because the Permanent Secretary was so outraged at not getting his own way.

So when it came to implementing the Welfare Consensus as Britain moved through the 1950s into the 1960s nobody doubted the pivotal role of the Civil Service in implementing it. And in the case of penal policy Radzinowicz tells us that: "The role played throughout by the core of the Home Office departments cannot be too highly emphasized. They provided the expertise and the balance" (Radzinowicz 1999, p 119). More than just that, they provided: "the red light when to stop and the green light when to start" (Radzinowicz 1999, p 119).

SOURCES OF ADVICE

Advisory committees

Of course, these large central departments of State—and the Home Office is regarded as one of the senior departments of State—have always sought outside "expert" help. In the early days as we have seen they employed engineers who were required to marshal the human and material resources needed to centralize, unify and standardize the newly nationalized prison system. However, as senior civil servants took over the running of the Prison Commission and ideas about treating offenders developed, the nature of the "experts" changed, as did the machinery through which they were consulted. Experts, as it were, became outsiders looking in, serving the Department through a myriad of Advisory Committees and Royal Commissions, some permanent, others *ad hoc*.

In the immediate postwar period arguably the most important permanent committee was the Advisory Council on the Treatment of Offenders (ACTO) which was appointed in 1944 and operated until the mid-1960s, when it was replaced (or re-modelled) after the collapse of the ill fated Royal Commission on the Penal System in 1966. Such advisory committees in their various incarnations would have had outside experts, usually from the judiciary, from interested pressure groups like the Howard League for Penal Reform and, as time went by, increasingly from the academic sphere.

Several things need to be remembered about these committees. The first is that they were pretty much dominated by men into the 1960s. The exceptions were high profile female public figures like Margery Fry—she was related to Sir Samuel Hoare, later Lord Templewood—and Dame Barbara Wootton, a senior academic. Second, they were largely metropolitan in their make up. For example, senior judges were, fairly inevitably, based in London, as were lobbyists Margery Fry and Barbara Wootton who had spent many years as a magistrate in the area covered by the London County Council. Others like Leon Radzinowicz were only a short train journey away in Cambridge. Neither of these things is very surprising. Women had a much more subordinate position than they do now, especially in public affairs,[2] and the British State was then—even more than it is now—a highly centralized apparatus where all roads led to Whitehall and Westminster. (For a list of the "great and the good" who served on these committees see Leon Radzinowicz (1999) who is punctilious about matters of rank and title.)

What may be more surprising to the outsider, however, is the third and most important characteristic of postwar Home Office committees, namely, that they were, at best, pretty much chaperoned by senior Home Office civil servants, at worst, controlled by them. For example, ACTO was chaired by the Permanent Under Secretary of State at the Home Office and other civil servants were in attendance from time to time. About her service on such bodies Barbara Wootton has observed that she can remember occasions when those civil servants present outnumbered outside advisors!

So these committees, with their closed and sometimes overlapping memberships, were under the thumb of the Home Office. To think otherwise is to be unrealistic. Some years ago Morgan wrote:

> It must never be forgotten that advisory committees are created by government. Though they may not be entirely the creatures of ministers or departments, no government is likely to tolerate the continued existence of an advisory body which consistently produces advice which, for whatever reason, the minister does not want to hear ... It would be politically naive to imagine that they could achieve more than a limited degree of independence from the ministry; that is not their political function.

(Morgan 1979, p 15)

Such a judgment may be "realistic", but it does place very real limits on the innovative potential of advisory committees. As Barbara Wootton observed, while these bodies may be prevented from political disasters they "themselves failed to foresee", there may be a certain loss of spontaneity and the temptation to keep in step with departmental policy may result in imaginative new proposals being stillborn (Wootton 1978, p 14).

---

[2]   There were many other extremely able, but less publicly visible, women in the Howard League and the Magistrates'Association at this time. Mrs Rackham, a Cambridge councillor, and Cicely Craven, whom Margery Fry first met at Oxford, immediately come to mind. Their history is currently being uncovered (Logan 2002). To a degree their work, particularly in the Magistrates' Association at a local level, helped to balance the male, metropolitan bias I describe.

A final characteristic of these committees was their closed nature. Their discussions were not only private, but for a while, even secret (Morgan 1979). For example, for the first ten years of its existence ACTO's reports were not normally published so it was even difficult for those with a real knowledge and interest in penal matters to know what was being proposed by this charmed inner circle. But what of other sources of advice?

Pressure groups

It has been argued that of the many bodies which modern governments rely upon for providing them with information and expertise about policy, and also, arguably more important, which governments need to persuade if they are to mobilize support for their policies, pressure groups are by far the most important. Government-pressure groups relationships are therefore said to be reciprocal, about far more than just representing special interests.

In the immediate postwar period the pre-eminent group in the field of penal reform was the Howard League. What were the origins of this group? Whom exactly did it represent? How did it stand in relation to other groups in the penal lobby? Just how influential and successful was it?

The League had been established in the 1860s in memory of John Howard, and had been roundly criticized towards the end of the nineteenth century for its timidity. It was later re-invigorated by an influx of middle class suffragettes, and then after 1914 by conscientious objectors, so that by the inter-war years it had become more of a force in the field of penal policy making and was on close (and cordial) terms with senior civil servants at the Prison Commission and the Home Office. For example, the Chairman of the Prison Commission, Sir Alexander Patterson, accepted an invitation to visit the League with the Permanent Secretary at the Home Office, Alexander Maxwell, to explain the government's thinking behind the Criminal Justice Bill (1938).

The League remained though, even after the war, a small, middle class group. Its active membership was almost wholly London based, comprising magistrates, lawyers, a number of other interested, liberally inclined, middle class professionals and influential Members of Parliament. But if its social base was narrow, its policy making base was even narrower, in the hands of a small executive committee of the great and the good—"the experts". Rose captured the League's ethos at this time remarkably well when he wrote:

> In fact, the membership do not very much want to formulate the League's policy. What they want is a body of experts who are prepared to press upon the authorities an attitude of mind with which the membership in general agree. This, very roughly, is that the treatment of offenders should be primarily reformative in nature, rather than merely punitive ... The details of how this is to be done, the membership is, by and large, prepared to leave to the officers and the Executive, rightly concluding that they should know what action to take.
>
> (Rose 1961, pp 264/265)

In exercising its influence the League was both discreet and moderate; it eschewed too much publicity and rarely made outright attacks on the Prison Commission or the Home Office. It thus kept the militant Prison Medical Council—formed by conscientious objectors after 1945—at arm's length and, while supporting the National Campaign for the Abolition of Capital Punishment in the 1950s (about which more later), it sought mechanisms to separate out its own activities from this high profile and politically boisterous campaign.

The close and somewhat overlapping membership of the various policy-making circles we have so far described is well illustrated by the First Offenders Bill (1958). The idea behind this originated in the Criminal Justice Act 1948 which stipulated that before a court could sentence an adolescent to prison it must first give reasons why other, non-custodial sentences had not been thought appropriate. The result of this was a dramatic, short term decrease in the number of adolescents sent to prison. This prompted the chairman of the Howard League, George Benson MP, to suggest to the Home Office that this provision might be extended to adult first offenders.

This possibility was looked at in some detail by the Advisory Council on the Treatment of Offenders which included in its members both Benson and his Howard League colleague, Margery Fry. The outcome of this was the First Offenders Bill which with government backing reached the statute book untroubled, having been piloted through the Lords by Viscount Templewood, one of the Howard League's several prestigious vice presidents, and taken through the Commons by Benson.

This close relationship continued through the 1950s well into the 1960s. For example, Sir Charles Cunningham, the Permanent Secretary at the Home Office who had been so outraged by Roy Jenkins, was later to recall:

> The Howard League, of course, is a body of long standing and it has a very high reputation. The Home Office always had the most cordial relations with the Howard League. At the time we are talking about [1957–1966] our objectives were in a sense the same because this was a period when the department was trying to emphasize the main object of penal treatment was rehabilitation rather than retribution ... I think it was the Howard League that at one time took the initiative in suggesting a committee of enquiry into short sentences of imprisonment, which led the Home Secretary to refer the problem to the Advisory Council on the Treatment of Offenders. We had close contact with Hugh Klare as secretary of the Howard League and of course the Home Secretary was constantly seeing George Benson, who was for many years the chairman.
>
> (Quoted in Davies 1985, pp 117/118)

What is of interest here, again, is not so much the details of what was said about the utility (or otherwise) of short sentences by ACTO, but rather the tone of the Permanent Secretary's remarks, the suggestion that the relationship between the Home Office and the League was so close that he was quite uncertain as to exactly who had taken this initiative!

Informality and public service

Such closeness should not suggest that the Prison Commission, the Home Office and the Howard League did not sometimes disagree. This would be a caricature of highly educated, intelligent men and women engaged in one of the most difficult areas of social policy. But it is to suggest that their disagreements were not about fundamentals, and that what disagreements there were would not be allowed to jeopardize the open and convivial channels of communication that had been established between the various parties.

Many of these channels were informal. Much policy making was what has been called "backstage" policy making (Bottoms and Stevenson 1992). The secretary of the Howard league might meet the chairman of the Prison Commission, Lionel Fox, at their London club for drinks or for an informal luncheon (Christoph 1962). Such meetings cemented friendships and reinforced feelings of personal solidarity. As Anthony Sampson pointed out about this period: "The Whitehall bureaucracies all have club-like ideas of corporate solidarity and London clubs are themselves an intrinsic part of the life of Whitehall" (Sampson 1962, p 66).

The "clubbable" nature of this metropolitan elite was striking, but so too was its sense of public duty. Leon Radzinowicz, a member of several government advisory committees and Royal Commissions, has described his service on such bodies:

> Twenty years is a big slice of one's professional life, but my work with councils was as fruitful and agreeable as one could hope for in this sombre field of criminal justice where, as a general rule, disappointments far exceed rewards ... It was a very civilized and congenial grouping. Our disagreements were few and they were always voiced in an atmosphere of mutual tolerance and courtesy. In those days I would go to London quite frequently and I would have a drink or luncheon with some of the members of the council ... occasions which invariably turned out to be friendly and useful.
>
> (Radzinowicz 1999, p 327)

There is a touch of *noblesse oblige* about this; it is easy to imagine Radzinowicz at the foot of the stairs at his own club, the Athenaeum, which also was very popular with senior judges at this time (*The Economist,* 15 December 1956). Yet in this passage, and throughout the Radzinowicz *memoire*, there is a strong sense of public service, duty even, albeit a patrician one. This bound together leading academics, senior civil servants, gifted amateurs like Hugh Klare and Margery Fry from the Howard League and interested backbenchers like George Benson in the search for more effective penal policies based less on Patterson's pre-war religious zeal and more on liberal humanism.

Duty, and yes, an exaggerated degree of their own self-importance, does comes across in this circle, but *public service rather than private gain* was the motive.

If this sounds too self-congratulatory it is worth remembering that by the mid-1960s this cosy, largely amateur world was being challenged, and one of the main protagonists was Radzinowicz himself. He had objected to the work of the Royal Commission on the Penal System (1966), announced in the Conservative government's White Paper, *The War Against Crime 1959–64* (1964), and to which he had been appointed. He took the view, and it helped eventually to sink the Royal Commission, that the way the Commission was going about its business was unprofessional. Instead of inviting round the usual suspects like the Howard League and the Archbishop of Canterbury to muse over the purposes of the penal system and then exchange a *pot pourri* of intelligent policy suggestions about the way forward, the Commission would be better served by employing young, professional field researchers to undertake work on its behalf to come up with "evidence-based" policy interventions.

It was partly as result of this critique, and following the demise of the Royal Commission, that ACTO was replaced by a new Advisory Council on the Penal System (ACPS) which was intended to be more professional in its approach, and to facilitate this more academics were invited to serve (Hood 1974). This change reflected not only the Radzinowicz critique, but also the growth of criminological research in Britain.

The government had established the Home Office Research Unit in the mid-1950s. This Unit was in daily contact with penal operatives in the field, so reflecting departmental priorities, while several universities received funds to promote more independent research. The government had given its blessing to the establishment of the Institute of Criminology at Cambridge in 1959, for example. The different roles of the Home Office research and university based research had been clearly set out in the government's White Paper, *Penal Practice in a Changing Society* (HMSO 1959, para 18). Thus by the mid-1960s criminological research in Britain was past the Cinderella stage; and the "gifted amateurs" had begun to be re-positioned. But this is to anticipate.

What I propose to do now is to examine the role of other "stakeholders" in the penal system in the immediate postwar decades. Having identified an inner, metropolitan elite that dominated the policy-making process at the centre, I now want to turn to the administration of the penal system itself, especially the prison system to explore what sort of world it was, and to discover what voice was given to those who actually ran the penal system, prison officers, governors and probation officers.

Were they without a voice? Were they too kept at a discreet distance, like the public? And what about the prisoners themselves, those who would today be included as among the system's "customers"? What were their rights?

THE PENAL SYSTEM

Operatives and professionals

Prison officers
When it came to major policy matters prison officers—referred to in the Home Office as "subordinate staff "—were almost entirely marginalized in the postwar years. Their attempts to unionize had always been bitterly resisted by government, and when they formed an "illegal" alliance with the police to take strike action in 1919 74 prison officers were immediately dismissed. Not until 1938 was the Prison Officers' Association (POA) formally recognized. Even then, however, the views of the Association were never taken seriously by the Prison Commission or the Home Office.

True, in the postwar period the POA was sometimes formally consulted by this or that advisory body. Such consultation is the nature of modern government as we have suggested, but J. E. Thomas has observed that during these years there was not a single occasion "when its views made the slightest difference" on any major issue (1977, p 68). For instance, in the mid-1960s the POA had wanted all high risk prisoners (category A prisoners as they were classified following the Mountbatten Report (HMSO 1966)) to be held in a single Alcatraz type prison. The Advisory Council on the Penal System advised against this strategy, and such, predictably, was the view accepted by government.

Prison officers, many recruited directly from the lower ranks of the armed forces, felt under a good deal of pressure in these postwar decades. At a basic level there were the usual concerns over pay and conditions, and talks on these matters went to arbitration on six separate occasions in the 1950s. Their role in the process of reform, limited though it might be, was seen to be threatened by specialists. For example, psychologists, who had been employed by the Prison Medical Service after 1946, were viewed with suspicion. They were seen as being more in sympathy with the views of prisoners than of prison officers who at the end of the day were left to do the "dirty jobs". This should not imply that these particular specialists were very influential outside their assessment wings. In spite of official rhetoric about their importance, in 1965 there were still only 19 psychologists in the entire prison system, including Borstals (Richards 1977). Like those educational professionals who were then coming on stream, they were pretty marginal in the overall scheme of things.

Prison governors
This subordinate role for prison officers is perhaps understandable given the liberal, progressive views of those making policy at the centre. After all, even its staunchest supporters would have to acknowledge that the POA had opposed just about every progressive reform over many years. But what of the governors? The direct entry system that encouraged the recruitment of progressive men and women into the service—often the men had held the King's or Queen's commission—was widely admired abroad. Surely governors were in a different category?

The short answer is that governors also exerted very little influence. In the first place, they were small in number, and their staff representation in those days was subsumed under the umbrella of the Society of Civil Servants. Second, they seem to have been a highly individualistic bunch, so mustering an agreed "governors' view" would probably have been a struggle. This was made more difficult by the fact that they were pretty much isolated from each other, rarely meeting as a body of governors. So when they did communicate with the Prison Commission it was mostly about administrative matters concerning their own prison or Borstal rather than about broader issues of policy (Thomas 1977). It is true that individual, charismatic governors like John Vidler at Maidstone prison had a public profile, but even he was said to be losing his room for manoeuvre in the 1950s as the Prison Commission exerted even more control from the centre (Heckstall-Smith 1954).

This isolation of prison governors was further exacerbated by the tendency of the new professional grades to look to, and work through, the centre rather than the governor as they had done in the past. Governors felt they were being bypassed, that they were less in control of "their" prisons then they used to be. The totally subordinate role of governors is captured by Joan Henry, whose account of her time in HMP Askham Grange tells how its respected governor, Mary Size, was peremptorily *summoned* to London to answer personally to the Commissioners after one of her charges absconded (Henry 1952).

It is perhaps instructive to note here that the Advisory Committee on the Penal System did not appoint anyone to its ranks with any really detailed knowledge of running prisons until 1976, and then it was a regional controller rather than serving governor. Governors who were responsible for the day to day administration of the system, apparently, had little to offer in strategic terms (Morgan 1979).

Prison doctors
The role of prison doctors is best understood in the context of the delivery of prison services generally. That is to say, services were then mostly provided inhouse from medical services to education. Outside professionals were mostly not needed, nor was their curiosity encouraged. Thus, the Prison Medical Service (PMS) was left outside the newly created National Health Service. Prisoners had no legal right of access to local practitioners, and any complaint by a prisoner against a doctor could not be dealt with by the Regional Health Authority, nor did prisoners come within the compass of the Community Health Authorities. Furthermore, professional bodies like the General Medical Council and the British Medical Association (BMA) adopted a hands off approach to prisons, rarely intervening. This not only left the issue of the quality of medical care hidden from scrutiny, it also left the crucial role of the prison doctor, the conflict between his duty to place health above the needs of discipline and of control, out of sight and out of mind (Sim 1990).

To compound this neglect, if anything did go fatally wrong with medical treatment there was little hope that an inquest—compulsory for deaths in custody—would uncover anything untoward since coroners' proceedings at that time were heavily skewed in favour of the prison authorities. Investigations into such deaths were carried out by seconded, or recently retired, police officers, while the lack of disclosure of information to bereaved families at inquest hearings protected the prison authorities from effective public scrutiny.

The world of the prison medical officer—many of them with military backgrounds at this time—was therefore largely unaccountable. It was professionally isolated and politically and judicially protected.

It is true that this professional isolation was recognized by the Prison Commission and the BMA and attempts were made to encourage the prison doctors to embrace the wider world of the behavioural sciences in order to understand the more "perplexing " questions behind individual criminal actions. This unfortunately led to some very questionable and largely unsupervised professional practices, including, as we move into the late fifties and sixties, the experimental use of psychotropic drugs for control purposes (Sim 1990).

Changes to the Prison Medical Service did reflect its growing importance. For instance, the new post of Director of Medical Services was created in the late 1940s. But the PMS was never a big player in the Commission (Sim 1990). The reason was simply that security and disciplinary concerns came first. As for local prison medics, they were too busy supporting the disciplinary staff to form a cohesive, professional pressure group. Sometimes they even sided with rank and file officers against the "mumbo jumbo" of prison psychologists. Trying to make the PMS credible and accountable had been one of the Prison Medical Reform Council's major objectives since the 1940s. Middle class conscientious objectors had been withering in their comments on prison medical officers in a survey interpreted for the Howard League by ex-offender Mark Benney (Benney 1948).

The Probation Service[3]
Elsewhere in the penal system the Probation Service was also moving towards a more psychiatric, case-work approach in the 1950s. With financial support from the Home Office probation officers began attending university courses. This considerably enhanced the professional status of the service which owed its origins to the work of church court missionaries at the turn of the twentieth century, and which was still continuing to recruit more or less directly from the armed services, as did the Prison Service. However, the National Association of Probation Officers (NAPO) was hardly a force to be reckoned with in the policy making process. It had only achieved independent negotiating status with government in 1942. Furthermore, not only were the numbers of probation officers at this time few, the service was also fragmented because officers were appointed by magistrates' committees and were technically servants of the local court rather than answerable to the Home Office.

The Home Office took a special interest in the Probation Service, it is true, but the relationship was a somewhat paternal one with government being very much the dominant partner (King and Jarvis 1977). The Probation Service, like the Prison Service, had to wait until 1976 before one of its senior officers was appointed to the Advisory Council on the Penal System.

So, it was very much a top down system, and J. E. Thomas's bitter complaint in the 1970s that "the powers that be" had little time for the opinions of those who ran the Prison Service in particular was a long running one (Thomas 1977, pp 71/72). This resentment had been publicly aired in 1963 when the Prison Commission was finally incorporated into the Home Office. The consolidation had originally been proposed in the Criminal Justice Act 1948. The Commission was thought by Whitehall to be an administrative anomaly, a Victorian "agency" which had to be brought more directly under central government control. This had been successfully resisted in 1948 on the grounds that a separate Commission offered both "identifiable leadership" and administrative expertise and continuity. There was a genuine concern about what might happen if the Commission was incorporated and administrative grade civil servants began floating in and out of the proposed Prison Department as if it were "just like any other department." But these arguments were swept aside in the early 1960s, and lobbyists like Hugh Klare were to find the State apparatus less porous than it had been, even less sensitive to the demands of those actually working the system.

Prisoners
Given that those who actually ran the Prison Service had little clout in policy making it is hardly surprising that its "customers" had even less of a voice. The very idea that a national prisoners' union was being mobilized would both have astonished and outraged the public, just as they would have been astonished to hear them described as "customers", let alone "stakeholders". True, at local level what was known as "the Norwich experiment" in the 1950s had involved prison staff/inmate councils, and this experiment had won government support, but the

---

[3]   Now, since 2001, re-branded the National Probation Service.

idea that ways must be found to safeguard prisoners' democratic rights would more than likely have met with the question, "What rights?"

The possibility that prisoners might have insights about their own experiences was not seriously considered. As Diana Medlicott has observed, accounts of prison life were mostly taken to reside in the official accounts of policy makers and statisticians. Historically, the voices of inmates had not been acknowledged as significant in debates about justice, sentencing or prison regimes. Rather than being seen as "subject" consumers of penal policy, they were all too often viewed as its "objects" (Medlicott 2000). Nothing better describes the situation of prisoners in the 1940s and 1950s than this. And even when it seems they did speak, prisoners were not to be believed. As the chairman of the Howard League was to phrase it deftly some years later, their accounts are "inherently unreliable" (Blom-Cooper 1977, p 9).

In this vein friends of the Prison Commission found a way of putting down Joan Henry's totally unsentimental account of her prison experience in the early 1950s by suggesting that it must be suspect if it was praised by *The Manchester Guardian* (Stokes 1957). Unfortunately we do not know what Stokes thought of the subsequent 1953 feature film which drew on her book and starred Diana Dors, but we do know that the book was also roundly condemned by the Howard League which leapt to the defence of the Prison Service by writing to *The Manchester Guardian* to condemn its alleged inaccuracies (Rose G 1961).

There are other ways to influence policy, of course. Trade unions like the POA, professional associations like NAPO and their equivalents may not have had formal policy making powers, but they could call strikes and organize demonstrations or work to rule. Prisoners in their turn could organize demonstrations, even "riot" on occasions. Such actions can have a significant impact on penal policy, as the Strangeways riot of 1990 would demonstrate.

It seems likely therefore that the prison "disturbances" at HMPs Portland (1950), Cardiff (1959) and Durham (1963) will have had some impact on Prison Commission thinking at this time, and following the rare intervention by an MP, the formidable Bessie Braddock from Liverpool, two prison officers were found guilty of ill treating inmates (*but not dismissed*). There was also a break out at the Carlton House Approved School in 1959 which became something of a *cause célèbre*.

We should also not lose sight of the obvious fact that beyond such major counter attacks, the day-to-day administration of prisons provides enormous scope for resistance. For example, prisoners took the work of psychotherapists with a long spoon in the 1950s and 1960s, and it is difficult not to believe that gay prisoners resented being "treated" for the "disease" of homosexuality. Making prison policy is one thing; implementing it is quite another. Subversion is endemic in totalitarian institutions; it is something that prisoners soon master, and prison staff learn to live with, understanding then as now, that order has to be negotiated.

SECRECY

It is likely that the extent of this routine resistance was under reported at the time. This was because the day-to-day workings of the prison system were shielded from the public. Just about all prison services were delivered inhouse. Furthermore, when prisoners had to attend court they were escorted there by prison officers. They later returned together, the prisoner to his cell, the prison officer to his on-site house or hostel. Prisons were a closed world, in a very real sense.

This isolation was reinforced by the Official Secrets Act that every prison officer had to sign. This was no token gesture. Officers felt quite constrained by it, forever frightened that in an unguarded moment they might let something slip on "security". Prison governors theoretically had more freedom, but on all sensitive issues they were instructed to get clearance from the Prison Department. A bland speech to the local Women's Institute on the progress of prison reform might have been risked, but a platform speech to the Howard League touching on policy matters: that would most certainly have required official clearance, and indeed, might have been prevented (Cohen and Taylor 1976).

The press was pretty much excluded from policy deliberations; the Home Office was almost a "no go" area. Indeed, it has been argued that governments then briefed journalists better on defence and foreign affairs than they did on penal policy (Dean 1977). Even when, after much pleading, journalists were allowed to write about the running of the penal system reporters were kept on a tight rein. If they dared to criticize, then there was usually an almighty row as the metropolitan elite closed ranks against what it identified as "ill informed" outsiders.

A very good example of this was the row that followed a 1950s press report into detention centres. We have seen that these centres had been provided for by the Criminal Justice Act 1948 to administer a "short, sharp shock" to young offenders. They were taken at the time to be a sop to opponents of the abolition of corporal punishment like Lord Goddard. A press story some years later in the *Daily Herald* about the operation of the centres at Kidlington and Goudhurst under the somewhat melodramatic heading "I call this BRUTAL" was highly critical, both of the daily regimes, and also the absence of any psychiatric or medical certification. The Prison Commission was outraged, and at first tried to ban the report, but the *Daily Herald* went ahead. What then happened was that the Howard League *summoned* the reporter before its executive committee and tried to find holes in her story, so hoping to destroy her credibility. But with the support of the *Daily Herald's* editor and some supportive letters from the public, Myrna Blumberg stood her ground (Ryan 1978).

What makes this episode particularly interesting is that the Howard League had been far from happy about how these centres were being run. Indeed, it had been *highly* critical. Yet when it came to outsiders rocking the boat it immediately stepped in to defend the service and those who ran it. Their criticism was one thing; intervention by "outsiders" on the other hand, that was another matter altogether. Whatever next? The public might start to take an interest, and who knew where that might end?

VICTIMS

Amid this talk about those who would now be regarded as "stakeholders" and "outsiders", it is instructive to consider the attention, or a lack of it, given to victims at this time. Not only were victims the other side of the offending coin, so to speak, but just who looked to their interests, and how they were attended to, illustrates the top down policy making process we are seeking to describe.

Victims could be looked at just like other subjects of the Welfare State. As the unemployed might need some form of insurance against unemployment, so might the victims of crime require some form of compensation against the misfortune which had befallen them through no fault of their own, and there is evidence that campaigners looked at the issue in this light. However, it has been argued that others, notably Margery Fry, managed this issue with a very different agenda. Her concern was more to demonstrate that penal reformers did care about victims, and not just criminals, and that a campaign to secure compensation for them might be used to buy off those who were still outraged against the abolition of corporal punishment. Put in a slightly different way, it might be the price required to keep the "hangers and floggers" at bay.

Whatever the motives, Margery Fry's skilful lobby to secure the Criminal Injuries Compensation Board had won over the Home Office by 1964 (Rock 1990). But what exactly were the needs of victims? Nobody asked victims, any more than they might have asked prisoners what they wanted. What they needed was decided by the "usual suspects" at the centre. As Rock has observed:

> The securing of a compensation scheme bore a marked resemblance to other successful projects of reform initiated at the same time … Those reformers were not pressed by any organization of the weak and the needy. They identified problems which they had themselves defined, and they behaved with considerable assurance. They were credible, authoritative, and respectable.
>
> (Rock 1990, p 89)

Victims had no more voice than prisoners in deciding things. The amount of money put aside for compensation, by the way, was very modest, and the terms on which it might be offered, highly restrictive around the notion of culpability. For example, prostitutes need not bother to claim for being beaten up by their clients. They would almost certainly be judged to have placed themselves in a vulnerable position and must take the consequences. Battered wives also need not apply as assailants living as members of the same family were expressly excluded. The compensation scheme also received very little publicity, so many eligible victims did not come forward.

THE PARTIES, PARLIAMENT AND THE PUBLIC

If the metropolitan elite guided by "experts" and pressure groups could marginalize or exclude penal operatives, professionals and even mostly gag the press, surely in a modern democracy they could not ignore the electorate and Parliament?

So what about members of the public more broadly defined? If we leave aside using newspapers, which in any case had their own axes to grind, what other channels (or mechanisms) were then available to ordinary people to convey their views on penal questions to those whom they had elected to govern?

These apparently simple questions raise a number of complicated issues which we will need to unpack in this and later essays. But let us make a start here by focusing on party activists.

Party activists

Local party associations, it is true, did send forward motions on a wide range of policy issues which were composited by party managers and then debated at Blackpool or Brighton. However, in the decades immediately following the war the Labour Party rarely discussed penal policy matters. What dominated Labour Party conferences immediately after the war were questions about economic management, funding the National Health Service and, later in the 1950s and early 1960s, the divisive issues of nuclear disarmament and Britain's membership of the European Union. Issues of high policy rather than penal policy were the order of the day.

The Conservative Party, on the other hand, did debate penal issues and the rhetoric was at times pretty punitive, more punitive than official government policy. However, it needs to be understood that these conferences were organized by the various Conservative and Unionist Associations in the country and represented their views. The Conservative Party in Parliament was constitutionally a different body and therefore could not be bound by any conference decisions (unlike the Labour Party, which was bound by its conference decisions, at least in theory). This gave the Conservative leadership the space to negotiate rank and file opinion on penal policy and to deflect its more punitive edge. True, this sometimes made conference appearances uncomfortable for liberal Home Secretaries like R. A. Butler, but this came as part of the territory and nobody expected that rank and file opinion would prevail; it might be politely listened to, but was unlikely to be translated into policy.

Outside of conferences, party members were at liberty to write to their Members of Parliament, as could any member of the public, and there is evidence that on issues of corporal and capital punishment many did so, even forcing special—and often heated—local meetings to discuss the issue (Christoph 1962). However, the conventions of British government meant that there was little hope of translating this grass roots opinion into policy as ordinary backbench members had little impact on routine policy making. This was basically the responsibility of the Executive, the Ministers advised by their civil servants and Whitehall advisory bodies and "experts".

Parliament might intervene now and again; it had, of course, to debate and pass the legislation that came before it, even though its passage was ensured by the party Whips. But basically the core machinery of British government was shielded from Parliamentary scrutiny at this time and Ministers were trusted to get on to do "their best". This trust, deference almost, to those in government, supported by legal sanctions preventing the press from interrogating Whitehall, was a widely-recognized aspect of our political culture. And lest we forget, constitutionally speaking they were the King's or Queen's Ministers in

Parliament, not the people's. The idea of Parliamentary Select Committees burrowing away in Whitehall departments like the Home Office, challenging government policy, publicly calling Ministers to account, was simply not entertained.

So, all in all, the leverage that ordinary citizens could apply through the formal political system on penal questions, or any other questions for that matter, was modest, even if they were party activists. How this combination of deference and privacy afforded governments the opportunity to manoeuvre around public opinion is well illustrated by returning in more detail to the controversial issues of corporal and capital punishment.

Two case studies: Corporal and capital punishment

Opinion polls tell us that re-introducing corporal punishment as a sentence of the courts had a decent level of support in the country at this time, and as we have seen, it was also supported by some members of the higher judiciary, many magistrates, and was pressed by Conservative party activists in the immediate postwar years. This pressure continued throughout the 1950s. At one point the Magistrates' Association campaigned for the reintroduction of the punishment under the banner: "Children of the nuclear age require robust punishment". Like Lord Chief Justice Goddard, the view was that a good whipping never did anyone any harm. In the early 1960s during the passage of the Criminal Justice Bill (1961) 57 Conservative backbenchers, including Mrs Thatcher, led a backbench rebellion in support of its reintroduction.

This put the government is some difficulty, and Home Office papers show that civil servants carefully monitored the activities of the Campaign for the Restoration of Corporal Punishment while considering their tactics. These were complicated by the wish of some Prison Commissioners to ban the use of corporal punishment in prisons as well. One option, that the Prison Commission might simply refuse to sanction the use of the punishment even where it was recommended, was seriously considered, but turned down by civil servants as too risky. The truth might just filter out and Parliament would feel it had been deceived (PCOM 9/984). So some formal constitutional restraints were acknowledged.

This led R. A. Butler to refer the issue to the Advisory Council on the Treatment of Offenders whose "experts" came to the conclusion that there was no firm evidence that corporal punishment had ever been a deterrent, and that its reintroduction would turn the clock back 100 years. Armed with this endorsement the government felt more secure, it could hold the line against public opinion and mobilize consent for abolition behind the penal *cognoscenti*. The struggle was all but over, public sentiment had been skilfully outmanoeuvred.

The Advisory Council's conclusion came as no great shock to any insiders at the time, nor should this surprise us given what we know of their operation. Had government anticipated any other conclusion it would simply not have referred the issue to the Council. (Even then, proponents of corporal punishment did not give in, and Home Secretary Roy Jenkins was criticized for stepping in to prevent the birching of a psychiatrically disturbed juvenile at Maidstone gaol in the mid-1960s (Jenkins 1975)). This strength of reaction probably explains why detention centres continued to be used long after they had much credibility among the *cognoscenti* (Land 1975).

The question of capital punishment was another example of where managing public opinion was again an issue, though securing a liberal outcome far was from certain. It was a subject on which everyone might make a moral judgment whatever the "experts" might come up with. Furthermore, deep fissures within the metropolitan elite appeared. But again, the Civil Service and advisory bodies played an important role in shaping the pace (and nature) of these compromises.

In terms of our argument the first thing to notice is that although the abolition of capital punishment was official Labour Party policy, the Permanent Secretary at the Home Office opposed legislating for its abolition in the Criminal Justice Bill (1947) because he felt public opinion was overwhelmingly hostile to it, and every opinion survey at the time supported this view. He also advised the Home Secretary that opponents of abolition included a large number of working class voters, and it was partly in deference to their views that Home Secretary Chuter Ede held back from including it in the 1947 Bill (Christoph 1962).

This was the senior Civil Service applying the red light, as Radzinowicz has put it, and Ede registered the signal. It was a reform too far. Ede was therefore unmoved when the Howard League presented a discreet petition from over 200 MPs in favour of debating abolition. More pressure was needed, but unwilling to risk damaging its close relationship with the Home Office, the League arranged that Roy Calvert's Council for the Abolition of the Death Penalty would rally support with public meetings and intense lobbying. This eventually paid off and Ede was forced to accept a free vote on an abolitionist clause put forward by Sidney Silverman.

The abolitionist debate was a grand Parliamentary occasion, with the abolitionists putting forward a cross bench team to make their cases. The public and press galleries were packed and the outcome of the debate eagerly awaited. The usual arguments were put forward. What right had anyone to take another life, least of all in the name of some abstraction, the State? What about the possibility, the likelihood even, that innocent people were hanged?

The outcome of the debate was far from certain, and the fact that someone claimed that Sir Alexander Patterson had joined the abolitionists may have persuaded some members, though certainly not the Home Secretary who again reminded the House, and his party in particular, that many working class people still favoured the death penalty. In the end the abolitionists won it, but by a very slender majority: 23 votes. Labour members were firmly in favour of abolition; the vast majority of Tories against.

However, the argument was not yet over. The abolitionist clause had still to go before the Lords who were known to be against it, and the retentionists took great heart from the fact that an opinion poll shortly after the Commons vote showed that whatever their elected representatives might say, people of all ages and all socio-economic groups remained firmly in favour of the death penalty. Armed with this evidence the Lords, led by Lord Goddard and other Law Lords, hurled themselves against the clause, defeating it overwhelmingly. A compromise clause to restrict capital punishment to certain categories of murders was then proposed, but it was clear that the game was up. The Labour government did not want a constitutional clash on this issue when it was trying to pilot its massive programme of postwar re-construction through Parliament, and certainly not on an issue which had only limited public support.

This Parliamentary struggle is of particular interest to us, of course, because it demonstrates that the policy making metropolitan elite which was responsible for steering penal policy in a modestly progressive direction after 1945 was itself divided over this reform, or at least its timing. This allowed other political elites in the Lords—largely hereditary at this time—to mobilize wider public opinion to hold up the pace of reform. In short, the tightly drawn, hands on, metropolitan elite which I have identified, did not have things all their own way in this period. Now and again a certain combination of political, constitutional and other circumstances conspired to give political clout to the public voice.

But the struggle was far from over. In order to defuse the issue the Labour government set up a Royal Commission, but was careful not to put abolition *per se* on the agenda. Instead it was asked to "consider and report whether liability under the criminal law in Great Britain to suffer capital punishment for murder should be limited or modified" (HMSO 1953). Abolition was not ruled out, but it need not be centrally addressed. In the event, the Commission came up with some interesting suggestions, not least that the jury might be given the responsibility of recommending that a defendant should be imprisoned if found guilty rather than being hanged. Inevitably this suggestion touched off a debate within the Commission about whether the defendant's "state of mind" at the time of the murder might be taken into account, and exactly what such a phrase might mean.

Other core issues were not addressed, simply knocked into touch, which is exactly what the government had intended. However, the publication of the Commission's report in 1953 did raise the issue again, though interestingly it was the controversial hangings of Derek Bentley, Timothy Evans and Ruth Ellis that really raised the public temperature. While these cases did not entirely blot out the more measured, objective debate surrounding the findings of the Royal Commission, they flamed the public imagination and inspired a continuing interest that was measurably more powerful than the deliberations of the great and the good. People argued over these cases in pubs, offices, and on the factory floor.

Derek Bentley had been involved in a robbery with Christopher Craig. They were disturbed and Craig killed the policemen trying to arrest him. Bentley was already in custody at the time of the shooting when he allegedly called to Craig to "Let him have it!", an ambiguous shout that could have been advice to Craig to let the approaching policeman have his gun, or an instruction to use it. However, because Craig was only 16 he could not be hanged, and so was sentenced to life imprisonment instead. Bentley on the other hand, was hanged, which many thought a great injustice.

The case of Timothy Evans was even more disturbing and shocking. Evans had been hanged for the murder of his wife Beryl and his young daughter. But some time later the bodies of six other women were found at his house and his lodger at the time, a former part-time policeman John Christie, who had earlier given evidence against him, admitted to the six murders, and that of Mrs Evans, though denying to the very end that he had murdered the daughter. The public felt that an entirely innocent man had been hanged, and Ludovic Kennedy's 10

Rillington Place (1961), an unusually hard hitting piece of journalism at the time, cast some dark suspicions over the conduct of the police enquiry and the subsequent trial.

The case of Ruth Ellis was very different. She had shot her lover dead and admitted her guilt. However, the feeling that she had been shabbily treated by a series of men who inhabited London's clubland, and the stoicism with which she conducted herself at her trial, led to much public sympathy. Her composure and calm presence appeared directly to challenge the claim by an expert witness called in her defence that "women are more prone to hysterical reactions than men" and that they tend to solve their problems in a more "primitive" way (Goodman and Pringle 1974; for an alternative reading, Ballinger 2000).

Public concern over these cases, and the passionate public arguments they generated, provided ammunition for the newly formed National Campaign for the Abolition of the Death Penalty which was led by three great postwar publicists, Victor Gollancz, Arthur Koestler and Canon John Collins (of the Campaign for Nuclear Disarmament (CND)). Branches of the campaign were set up around the country, public meetings organized and Arthur Koestler published his highly influential *Reflections on Hanging* (1956). Professional or informed interest was also canvassed and the campaign could point to new and important allies. For example, in July 1955 *The Lancet* carried a powerful leading article which claimed:

> The death penalty seems as grotesque as did the witchcraft laws to eighteenth-century Englishmen. The feeling against it has been intensified by three notorious executions ... that of Evans, who may not have been guilty of the crime for which he was hanged; that of Bentley, who was not guilty of shooting but of shouting ... and that of Ruth Ellis, hanged for a murder done in a state of acute jealousy.

(The Lancet, 23 July 1955)

The rising level of public interest forced the government to acknowledge that the issue was not going to go away, and in 1956 it sought to steal a march on the abolitionists by bringing forward its own motion to change the law on murder without outlawing hanging. This compromise was rejected, however, and in 1956 the government was more or less forced into allowing Sidney Silverman to introduce a Private Member's Bill which, accompanied by much extra Parliamentary activity organized by the National Council, passed through the Commons by 210 votes to 120. But again the Lords threw out the Bill, this time by over 150 votes.

This put the Conservative government in a difficult position. It was not itself committed to abolition; on the other hand, it could not ignore the vote in the Commons and the possibility that it might have to invoke the Parliament Act 1948 to bypass the Lords, a very contentious step. In the event a compromise was achieved in the form of a Bill in two parts.

The first amended the law on murder, doing away with for example the doctrine of constructive malice which had sent Derek Bentley to the gallows, while the second part divided murders into "capital" and "non-capital". The former carried the death penalty, the latter did not. This distinction was not new, and was bound to throw up all sorts of anomalies, as had been pointed out a by a number of campaigners on both sides of the debate. However, the compromise was forced on the abolitionists and the measure eventually got through Parliament as the Homicide Act in March 1957. It was not particularly welcomed by either side, nor was it wholly endorsed by judges who had to engage with its ambiguities, but it set in train a series of manoeuvres which eventually led to complete abolition in 1967.

LEGITIMIZING THE FEW

The long struggle to secure abolition is evidence that the public—pro and anti hanging—did sometimes manage to make its opinion count, and we should never forget these moments. It also provides us with a convenient starting point to explore the arguments of those politicians, civil servants and lobbyists who were determined to subordinate public opinion on penal questions, and many other difficult questions for that matter.

We have noted that the cases of Derek Bentley, Timothy Evans and Ruth Ellis stirred public opinion. It was this that had led Silverman and his supporters to try again in 1955. They believed that public opinion was now flowing strongly in their favour. The moody crowd outside Holloway prison on the day Ruth Ellis hanged—about 1,000 people turned up on that July day in 1955—was taken as some proof of this.

In fact, this was a misconception. There was a slight swing in favour of abolition, but nothing like sufficient to change the overall picture. But it was nonetheless *believed* to be the case (Block and Hostetler 1998; Christoph 1962).

This prompted Silverman to table a Parliamentary question in November 1955 asking whether or not the Prime Minister had any plans to ascertain public opinion on capital punishment, to which a senior civil servant drafted a interesting reply which advised the Prime Minister to say: "I do not think it is necessary or desirable to take any steps to ascertain the state of public opinion" (PRO HO 291/95).

Further advice was pencilled in by the civil servant in case of a supplementary question from Silverman calling for a re-think. This advised:

> If it is suggested that there might be anything in the nature of a referendum the reply might be that it [is] the government's duty to reach its own decision, subject only to its responsibility to Parliament. Public opinion can and should be expressed through the ordinary constitutional channels ... the House would not wish any steps to be taken which would reduce its own importance as the means of focusing public opinion.

> (PRO HO 291/95)

Anything "in the nature of" I take to be a coded reference to the growing use of "opinion polling", particularly on the issue of capital punishment. The possibility of public consultation through a referendum was again ruled out in 1955, this time after discussion in Cabinet (PRO HO 291/93). The referendum was then seen by the British political class as a dangerous *populist* tool which continental dictators used to manipulate popular opinion rather than represent it through Parliament (Goodhart 1971).

The advice to the Prime Minister in November 1955, and the exchanges which followed it in Parliament, illustrated just how passionately those in government subscribed to a very traditional view about Parliament's role in Britain's great unwritten constitution.

Parliament was taken to be the sounding board for the nation. It should reflect various strands of public opinion and the government was obliged to listen to these opinions, should follow debates in the press and so forth; the archival evidence is that the Home Office did this, *but at the end of the day, the government made policy which Parliament was then invited to endorse*, or not, as the case may be.

The public was only involved *indirectly*. Government was taken to be a complex, difficult business requiring skill and judgement, and senior politicians should be allowed to get on with it. This applied to penal policy as much as it did to economic policy. Politicians were directly accountable to the public in general terms, of course, but this was only once every five years when the electorate was invited to chose between competing teams of leaders.

Legitimizing this modest role for the people in government had been the task of nineteenth-century political educators like John Stuart Mill. It was an attempt by the educated classes to come to terms with what Ortega y Gasset (1951) has described as the "rise of the masses", the birth of western democracies that had extended the franchise to the uneducated and unleisured. About such people and their role in government Mill reassured his readers:

> It is not necessary that the many should themselves be perfectly wise, it is sufficient if they be duly sensible of the value of superior wisdom. It is sufficient if they be aware, that the majority of political questions turn upon considerations of which they, and all persons not trained for the purpose, must necessarily be imperfect judges; and that they must in general be exercised rather upon the characters and the talents of the persons whom they appoint to decide those questions for them, than upon the questions themselves.
>
> (J S Mill, quoted in Williams 1976, p183)

Thus:

> The true idea of representation is not that the people govern in their own persons, but that they chose their governors. In good government public questions are not referred to the suffrages of the people themselves, but to those of the most judicious whom the people can find. The sovereignty of the people is essentially a delegated authority. Government must be performed by the few, for the benefit of the many.
>
> (J S Mill, quoted by J H Burns 1968, p 264)

What this translated into is that Parliament should "control government, question it, supervise it, criticize it ... but not itself govern. Legislation is a matter for experts and Parliament is there chiefly to represent opinions ..." (Williams 1993, p xxxvii). So, *both* the people *and* Parliament must understand their subordinate roles.

As the nineteenth-century revolution in government gathered pace, key among "the few" were higher civil servants, the Civil Service having been established on a permanent, competitive basis by the Northcote Trevelyan Report in the 1870s. It was they, in association with outside "experts" consulted for the knowledge that they could bring to the various services provided by government, and those senior politicians chosen for their judgment by Parliament to serve as ministers, who would give broad direction to the Whitehall machine. This represented the fusion of bureaucratic power with knowledge and political statecraft: the art of the possible.

It is important to note that "experts" did not rule. To be sure, in modern complex societies they had a crucial role to play, and none understood this better than Labour's Harold Laski. His Fabian pamphlet extolled the expert, claiming that issues in social policy should go "to an expert in social questions". Yet at the same time Laski warns that "experts" sometimes sacrifice the insight of "common sense" to pure intellect. This missing ingredient is provided by senior bureaucrats and experienced politicians (ministers). It is they who understand better the realities of delivering services than "experts", or the "plain man" for that matter, and it is they who appreciate the need to mobilize consent, as no modern democratic government can maintain a social policy for long which runs "counter to the wishes of the multitude" (Laski 1935, p 12).

Deference

Mill's normative nineteenth-century view of how the democratic government *should work*, was a pretty good description of how British government *did work* in the two decades after 1945. Government was accepted as a top down, insider business. I have already suggested that this way of doing business was underpinned by a strong sense of deference, even trust, towards governing elites.

Gabriel Almond and Sydney Verba confirmed this in their comparative study of political attitudes towards democracy in the late 1950s and early 1960s. They suggested that deference was an identifiable and distinctive aspect of British civic culture, arguing persuasively that Britain was a much more "subject" orientated, top down society, then the "participant" orientated bottom up society of the United States. Indeed, they went so far as to argue that the balance between the "subject" orientated and the "participant" orientated aspects of our culture, as they had defined and measured it, was arguably too heavily in favour of the former.

This was not a threat to government. On the contrary, it meant a strong respect for government institutions like Parliament and the Civil Service, but it gave pretty much a free rein to dominant elites:

> One can argue that the balance in Britain is tilted too far in the opposite direction. It is possible that deference to political elites can go too far, that the strongly hierarchical patterns in British politics—patterns that have often been criticized as limiting the extent of democracy in that nation—result from a balance weighted too heavily in the direction of the subject and deferential roles.

(Almond and Verba 1963, p 494)

The sophisticated point being made by Almond and Verba here is that all societies have "subject" as well as "participant" elements in their civic culture which we can do our best to measure, it was just that as far as they could see, from an American perspective, these had tilted too much towards the former in Britain.

It might mean strong government. Indeed, British government was then credited by Almond and Verba as having one of the strongest executives among modern democracies, but this had its down side. When, for example, it was reinforced by a strong Official Secrets Act, government was a very private business indeed. As Richard Rose was to phrase it as late as 1965:

> Because there is trust in the good intentions of governors, it is possible for public figures to make public policy in considerable privacy. This privacy is strengthened by strong legal sanctions against those revealing unpublished government documents, and by strong cultural sanctions upholding the privacy of governmental deliberations.
>
> (Rose R 1965, p 43)

Seen in this wider context, the manner in which penal policy was made and administered in England at this time was not exceptional. Home Secretaries were held accountable at Question Time in the Commons every two or three weeks, and that was about the limit of scrutiny. True, this private practice was further reinforced in the case of penal policy by the fear of a punitive public culture. For example, Sir Lionel Fox and Hugh Klare were always conscious of this in their "backstage" dealings in the 1950s, and it was a sentiment publicly echoed some years later by Blom-Cooper of the Howard League who warned his audience:

> There are dangers in a pressure group in the penal field of broadening its appeal to the public in general. The subject of penal reform does not instinctively strike a sympathetic cord with large members of the public.
>
> (Blom-Cooper 1977, p 7)

While this may or may not have been true, the closed nature of penal policy making was only tolerable in the context of a wider political culture identified by Almond and Verba that encouraged those in power get on with the business of government pretty much untroubled, even escaping culpability when sometimes they deserved blame.

Explaining this unusual degree of deference, and understanding the protection it offered to those who wielded government authority, is no easy matter, any more than it is easy to define and then measure other components of our civil culture at this time. However, part of the answer surely lies in the fact that Britain was (and still is for that matter) an old, not to say "antique State", to borrow Tom Nairn's telling phrase (Nairn 1979), which has enjoyed long continuity, and where the incorporation of the masses into the political system was accomplished not by revolution, but by evolution, and where large sections of the working classes—Disraeli's angels in marble (Mackenzie and Silver 1968)—gave votes to the Conservative Party trusting that its leaders were, to borrow again from Mill, among the "most judicious".

This deference was complemented (and compounded) by a non-revolutionary Labour Party imbued with a strong technocratic bias from its

Fabian roots. This was respectful of the State, never doubting in the 1940s and 1950s, for example, that powerful but "neutral" civil servants could be trusted to deliver the Welfare State which its formal political emancipation demanded, nor ever really believing that the national party was the embodiment of the Rochdale Cooperative Society, whatever its constitution might suggest about the primacy of conference votes (Crick 1968).

Challenging the machinery of government was, therefore, simply not part of the mainstream political agenda in postwar Britain. Nor until we get into the late 1950s and early 1960s was there much public comment on the curious pattern of accommodation which had taken place between various elites that had characterized the peaceful evolution of modern British democracy.

So it was not seen as particularly risky, or atavistic as it might now seem, for the Conservative Party to have appointed a hereditary peer as its leader in 1963 to fight the General Election against the Labour Party led by a "meritocratic" grammar school boy, Harold Wilson. Conservative leaders were then still appointed by soundings, of course, and not voted for, and even when this changed later in the 1960s, the choice was given to the party in Parliament and not to the party in the country. Nor should it be forgotten that Labour's controversial *Crime: A Challenge to Us All* (Labour Party 1964) was overseen by another hereditary peer, Lord Longford. Political and social elites coexisted.

As late as 1961 there were still six old Etonians in Macmillan's Cabinet, 15 of whom went to Oxbridge, which was where most senior civil servants had also been educated (Sampson 1962). True, things were changing: life peers had been introduced by Macmillan in 1961 and Lord Home lost to Harold Wilson in the 1964 General Election, though only by the slenderest of margins. But in the postwar years, certainly in the immediate the postwar period, Labour, including Labour's own aristocrats from the trade union movement, co-existed in a very British way with the remnants of the old ruling class, and the meritocracy in the form of the Civil Service, to offer strong, confident, corporate government from the centre.

It needs to be remembered too, that this confidence in government had been boosted by the war. Britain had stood alone in Europe and, with Commonwealth and American support, had defeated Fascism. The resilience of its Parliamentary institutions had been demonstrated. Indeed, Britain was busy exporting the "Westminster model", as it was known in textbooks, around the world to the most unlikely places. In this climate it was quite appropriate that Hugh Klare should be invited by the Prison Commission to advise overseas governments on penal matters. Likewise, it was appropriate that British diplomats and lawyers should have drawn up a Convention On Human Rights to ensure the Rule of Law prevailed in continental European countries as a barrier to totalitarian rule.

Of course, we in Britain did not need to sign such a convention, or make provision for our subjects to petition Strasbourg. Our criminal justice system was among "the best and the fairest in the world". We had no need to guard or enshrine the legal rights of defendants or prisoners in this way. We could rely on the courts to defend these rights, just as they could be trusted to defend the citizen against any uncharacteristic administrative abuses of government.

Underpinning this postwar ideological confidence in the institutions was material affluence. The British people were told in 1957 that they had "never had it so good". Nor had most of them, and this was to continue. Between the early 1950s and 1970s Britain's economic performance had been more than just creditable. Real output, and output per worker, had increased faster than at any time since the mid-nineteenth century. Furthermore, there was remarkably low unemployment, the scourge of the interwar years, and low inflation (Feinstein 1994). Poverty became, almost, the forgotten Englishman. It was even argued that a process of *"embourgeoisement"* was at work. We were all on the way to becoming middle class, and the "end of ideology" was just around the corner.

It is hardly surprising that this perception induced confidence in government, in those who ran it, and in its processes, across a broad range of policies. The fact that government was top down business hardly seemed to matter. Most ordinary people did not appear to feel greatly patronized or threatened by it, and where "snobbishness" raised its head, and it frequently did, this was more associated with manners than politics.

CONCLUSION

When trying to take the pulse of the penal system in the first two decades of the postwar period, formal reports, particularly those annually compiled by the Prison Commission, need to be set against more realistic accounts. Joan Henry's description of prison life in HMP Holloway and at HMP Askham Grange (see above) and Heckstall-Smith's *Eighteen Months* (1954) are such accounts.

Clearly homophobic, probably racist, Heckstall-Smith had an instinctive dislike for the working classes. He agreed with Lord Goddard that they should be flogged to maintain social discipline. So this middle class war veteran who had been imprisoned for aiding and abetting a very serious fraud is not a very appealing witness, to me at least. However, I find his account of the brutalities perpetuated at HMPs Wormwood Scrubs and Maidstone mostly convincing. He explicitly derides the upbeat claims of Prison Commissioners like Lionel Fox who constantly assured the Howard League that education and training were now in place in our prisons. Ironically, and tellingly, Maidstone was designated and acclaimed as a training prison under Governor Vidley (Mark Benney's comments suggest that the regime at Wormwood Scrubs had long been a harsh one, though apparently, not the worst (Benney 1948)).

Another realistic account, in my view, is the by now classic sociological study of HMP Pentonville by Terence and Pauline Morris. Although "edited" under the provisions of the Official Secrets Act before it was finally allowed to go into print in 1963, the research—it had begun as early as 1958—revealed that violence was seldom far below the surface at Pentonville, and the official view that many of its prisoners were being rehabilitated was judged to be "pious optimism" (Morris and Morris 1963, p 266).

The public was partly complicit in sustaining the official deceit that our prisons were half-decent places. There was, for example, an unspoken understanding between it and the prison authorities that to maintain order and stability within the prison system an element of penal repression, verging at times on unrestrained violence by prison officers, was necessary. Provided this was carried out discreetly, then the civil servants and politicians who oversaw the prison system would not be expected to pry too closely into allegations of brutality. Nor would they worry too much if medical or other prison "standards" slipped.

However, this complicity was only sustainable in a system which was pretty much closed, where information about what was really going on was restricted, and where there was a widespread acceptance that the government could be safely left to "the few." Decent prison officers who were tempted to speak out against these practices were mostly silenced. And we should not forget that there were decent officers, as there were tolerable prisons. The few prison biographies I have had space to mention are testimony to this unevenness.

Overall however, the penal landscape in this period was much bleaker than the reformers would have had us believe. The reality is that prisoners were still slopping out in crumbling, often violent, local prisons, their mail was still being heavily censored, and in many prisons no constructive work was provided; confidence in the potential of juvenile institutions, especially Borstals, to reform was fast collapsing; the search for alternatives to prison had been unimaginative and tardy, while the struggle against capital punishment was compromised at the final hurdle.

This interpretation of penal policy and penal policy making in the postwar decades may seem to be ungenerous in a number of ways.

It suggests a small coterie of somewhat self-satisfied, well connected middle class, mostly male, metropolitan reformers, academics and a few sympathetic judges, sharing authority with powerful civil servants and ministers in pursuit of their own private agendas. These people were the ones who really counted when it came to making penal policy, not those who ran the penal system, prison governors or probation officers, or the public, let alone prisoners. Even Parliament was kept at a none too respectful distance. Furthermore, it suggests that the gains secured were more modest than these reformers might like to claim, that to locate their success in the broader picture of welfare reform at this time is to overstate their achievement, that punishment was not much blunted by welfare.

I acknowledge that this is indeed an unflattering picture. But it does not deny that some things were better than they once were. There was, for example, more association and less surveillance on the inside, a new psychiatric facility at Grendon Underwood had been announced in 1959 and as the Maxwell Committee (1953) noted, the Welfare State was now giving more practical help to prisoners on discharge.

Nor does this account deny that, arguably, things might well have been far worse had this coterie not existed at all. Still less does it interrogate the complex motives of those engaged in the business of penal reform, its satisfactions and frustrations. Nevertheless I am sure they would all have embraced, as I do, Lord Longford's noble, liberal sentiment at the time that while no one can demand mercy as a right, it is a mean person who never shows compassion and "a mean society that never exercises it" (Labour Party 1964, p70).

However, the opportunities offered by the moment of social calm underwritten by the historic compromise between capital and labour to secure a reduction in the general level of penal repression were not over exploited, to put it mildly. I can offer no easy explanation for this state of affairs. The argument that it was as far as the reformers could go, that they deserve more credit than I give them for managing a hostile public as successfully as they did in securing at least some worthwhile improvements, has some merit, I agree. It is even some sort of defence, if a defence is needed. It does seem to me, however, that this line of argument begs a prior condition, and that is this one.

The very nature of the policy making process at this time excluded experiences and critiques that were necessary to make better sense of penal practice. These experiences and critiques were the first requirement for upgrading the public debate, to give it authenticity and a sharper intellectual edge. The public needed to understand, for example, that in spite of what the Prison Commissioners might tell it, prison reform belonged more to the world of official discourse than reality. Without this input significant policy changes were unlikely. The existing, intellectually closed and hugely complacent policy making environment is wonderfully captured in the remarks of yet another Home Office Permanent Secretary who, looking back on the early 1960s, said to his invited audience at the Cambridge Institute of Criminology:

> It would be worth asking how much the analysis and proposals in *Crime—A Challenge to Us All* [1964] owed to their specifically political origin ... it seems unlikely that many of the proposals would have been viewed at the time as fiercely partisan, or as remote from continuing departmental objectives. The proposals clearly owed much to members of the group of course, but also to the generally available sources of expertise or received wisdom—the penal services themselves, the legal and academic communities, the various reform bodies and interest groups and a quantity of published official material.
>
> (Moriarty 1977, p 132)

In short, as far as those who ran the government machine were concerned everybody who needed to be consulted was being consulted during these years, and what is more, among the *cognoscenti* there was a consensus; there were no genuinely new, critical voices.

This self-congratulation was deeply ingrained. Those who made penal policy could not think themselves out of it, *nor could they be expected to*. What was required was a disruption of the wider, social democratic political consensus which challenged the authority of the State and undermined our entrenched feelings of deference towards those who ran the great Leviathan from Whitehall; it was only when this wider political challenge came in the second half of the 1960s that penal perspectives began to be radically examined and other voices began to be heard, including those of prisoners and women. What engineered this disruption, and the almost impertinent intrusion of these outsiders into the penal policy making process is something I want to both investigate and assess in my second essay.

REFERENCES for *Part I*

Almond G. and Verba S. (1963) *The Civic Culture* (New Jersey: Princeton University Press)

Ballinger A. (2000) *Dead Women Walking* (London: Ashgate)

Benney M. (1948) *Gaol Delivery* (London: Longman)

Block B. P. and Hostetler J. (1997) *Hanging in the Balance: A History of the Abolition of Capital Punishment in Britain* (Winchester: Waterside Press)

Blom-Cooper L. (1977) "The Role of Pressure Groups and Voluntary Organizations in Penal Reform" in Walker N. (ed.) *Penal Policy Making in England* (Cambridge: Institute of Criminology)

Bottoms A. and Stevenson S. (1992) "What Went Wrong? Criminal Justice Policy in England and Wales, 1945–1970" in Downes D. *Unravelling Criminal Justice: Eleven British Studies* (Basingstoke: Macmillan)

Burns J. H. (1968) "J. S. Mill On Democracy" in Schneewind J. B. (ed.) *Mill: A Collection of Critical Essays* (London: Macmillan)

Christoph J. (1962) *Capital Punishment and British Politics* (London: Allen and Unwin)

Cohen S. and Taylor L. (1976) *Prison Secrets* (London: NCCL and Radical Alternatives to Prison)

Crick B. (1968) "Them and Us: Public Impotence and Government Power" *Public Law,* Spring, pp 8–27

Dean M. (1977) "The News Media's Influence in Penal Policy", in Walker N. (ed.) *Penal Policymaking in England* (Cambridge: Institute of Criminology)

Feinstein C. (1994) "British Economic Growth since 1948" in Floud R. and Mcloskey D. (eds.) *The Economic History of Britain since 1870* (Cambridge: Cambridge University Press)

Garland D. (1985) *Punishment and Welfare* (Aldershot: Gower)

Garland D. (1900) *Punishment and Modern Society* (Oxford: Clarendon)

Goodhart P. (1971) *Referendum* (London: Stacey)

Goodman J. and Pringle P. (1974) *The Trial of Ruth Ellis* (Newton Abbot: David and Charles)

Heckstall-Smith A. (1954) *Eighteen Months* (London: Wingate)

Henry J. (1952) *Who Lie in Gaol* (London: Gollancz)

HMSO (1944) *Social Insurance and Allied Services* (Cmd 6404)

HMSO (1953) *Royal Commission on Capital Punishment 1948–1953* (Cmd 8932)

HMSO (1964) *The War Against Crime* (Cmnd 2296)

HMSO (1959) *Penal Practice in a Changing Society* (London: Home Office) Cmnd 645

HMSO (1966) *The Report of the Inquiry into Prison Escapes and Security by Earl Mountbatten* (Cmnd 3715)

Hood R. (ed.) (1974) *Crime, Criminology and Public Policy* (London: Heinemann)

Jenkins R. (1975) "On Being a Cabinet Minister" in Alt J. E. and Herman V. (eds.) *Cabinet Studies: A Reader* (London: Macmillan)

Kennedy L. (1961) *Ten Rillington Place* (London: Pan)

King J. F. S. and Jarvis F. (1977) "The Influence of the Probation and Aftercare Service" in Walker N. *Penal Policymaking in England* (Cambridge: Institute of Criminology)

Labour Party (1964) *Crime: A Challenge to Us All* (London: Labour Party)

Land H. (1975) "Detention Centres: the Experiment which Could not Fail" in Hall P., Land H., Parker R. and Webb A. *Change, Choice and Conflict in Social Policy* (London: Heinemann)

Laski H. (1935) *The Limitations of the Expert* (London: Fabian Society)

Lewis D. (1997) *Hidden Agendas* (London: Hamish Hamilton)

Logan A (2002) *Making Women Magistrates: Feminism, Citizenship and Justice in England and Wales 1918-1950* (Unpublished)

Mackenzie W. J. M. and Grove J. W. (1957) *Central Administration in Britain* (London: Longman)

Mackenzie W. J. M. and Silver A. (1968) *Angels in Marble* (London: Heinemann)

McLeod R. (1988) *Government and Expertise: Specialists, Administrators and Professionals* (Cambridge: Cambridge University Press)

Medlicott D. (2000) *Surviving the Prison Place* (London: Ashgate)

Morgan R. (1979) *Formulating Penal Policy* (London: NACRO)

Morris T. and Morris P. (1963) *Pentonville. A Sociological Study of an English Prison* (London: Routledge)

Morris T. (1989) *Crime and Criminal Justice since 1945* (Oxford: Blackwell)

Moriarty M. (1977) "The Policy Making Process: How it is Seen from the Home Office" in Walker N. (ed.) *Penal Policy Making in England* (Cambridge: Institute of Criminology)

Nairn T. (1979) *The Breakup of Britain* (London: New Left Books)

Ortega Y Gasset (1951) *The Revolt of the Masses* (London: Unwin)

Pollard S. (1992) *The Development of the British Economy 1914–1990* (London: Edward Arnold)

Radzinowicz L. (1999) *Adventures in Criminology* (London: Routledge)

Richards B. (1977) "Psychology, Prisons and Ideology: the Prison Department Psychological Service" *Ideology and Consciousness,* Autumn 1972, No. 2, pp 9–25

Rock P. (1990) *Helping Victims of Crime* (Oxford: Clarendon)

Rose G. (1961) *The Struggle for Penal Reform* (London: Stevens)

Rose R. (1965) *Politics in England* (London: Faber and Faber)

Ryan M. (1978) "The Acceptable Pressure Group" *Inequality in the Penal Lobby: a Case Study of the Howard League and Radical Alternatives to Prison* (Farnborough: Teakfield)

Sampson A (1962) *Anatomy of Britain* (London: Hodder and Stoughton)

Sim J. (1999) *Medical Power in Prisons* (Milton Keynes: Open University Press)

Stokes S. (1957) *Come To Prison* (London: Longman, Green and Co.)

Templewood Viscount (1954) *Twelve Troubled Years* (London: Collins)

Thomas J. E. (1972) *The English Prison Officer since 1850* (London: Routledge and Kegan Paul)

Thomas J. E. (1977) "The Influence of the Prison Service" in Walker N. (ed.) *Penal Policy Making in England* (Cambridge: Institute of Criminology)

Williams G. (1976) ed. *John Stuart Mill on Politics and Society* (London: Harvester)

Williams G. (ed.) (1993) *John Stuart Mill. Utilitarianism, on Liberty, Considerations on Representative Government* (London: Everyman/Dent)

Wootton B. (1978) *Crime and Penal Policy* (London: Allen and Unwin)

PART II

Outsiders

In this second essay I undertake what might best be described as a form of mobile archaeology.

I move across a number of different sites where penal policy was debated between the late 1960s and mid-1980s to uncover some of the social, political and intellectual forces (and movements) which came together to challenge both the way in which penal policy was made in England and Wales, and the intellectual and political foundations on which that policy rested.

Excavating these sites does not reveal a single narrative. Indeed, there were several narratives at work, sometimes overlapping, sometimes even conflicting. But my contention is that together they managed to build an informed and credible opposition to those elites which had dominated penal policy making since 1945, and whose activities, policies and policy making structures were outlined in my first essay.

Later I will attempt the far more difficult business of trying to assess the impact of this opposition. I want to ask not only how successful was it in making its several voices heard, but also to judge if it succeeded in any modest way in shifting the direction of official penal policy. It is one thing to mount a challenging critique, it is another matter altogether to get that critique listened to and then translated into government policy.

The factors underpinning this challenge came from outside the penal system itself as the consensus in British society was undermined and some previously deferential subjects began to demand a say in regulating their own affairs, claiming bodies of knowledge that were more authentic than those of the "experts" whose social engineering had let them down.

I start by exploring this wider context.

BREAKING WITH THE POSTWAR CONSENSUS

While the portrayal of Britain in the decades after 1945 as an increasingly prosperous, but deferential society, at ease with its top down style of government and trusting of those metropolitan elites who steered the great ship of State from Whitehall, is an accurate one in its essentials, we should not lose sight of dissenting voices and some cracks in the façade. To put the same thing another way, there was a consensus that all was well, but in the nature of things this was never complete, not least when it came to issues of social discipline.

For example, the campaign to re-introduce corporal punishment as a sentence of the court was fuelled in the 1950s by the development of a vibrant youth sub-culture around the Teddy Boys. The impression given in the press was of affluent young men in Edwardian dress, velvet collars, drainpipe trousers and boot lace ties, marauding our city centres in rival gangs, disrespectful of authority, and far too willing to produce the "flick knife" or the "cosh" (Pearson 1983). This was the "rock'n roll" generation, those who supposedly abandoned youth clubs, preferring instead to smash up dance halls from which they were frequently banned. This essentially working class phenomenon, partly explained at the time by affluence, partly by the weakening of family discipline, had a profoundly disturbing effect on an otherwise settled political order which was gearing up to enjoy the new prosperity.

Equally threatening, and not least because it was more obviously middle class and politically conscious, was the Campaign for Nuclear Disarmament (CND) which held its first protest march between Aldermaston and London in 1958. The campaign was significant for a number of reasons, but not least because while it sought to influence the established political parties, especially the Labour Party, it was also prepared to mobilize people, many of them young people, including the new generation of angry playwrights, artists and poets, in their tens of thousands *outside* the established political framework to protest against the arms race.

This extra-Parliamentary activity was deeply worrying to those in authority. Its disregard of the "usual channels" was met with panic and the heavy handed use of the law in 1961 when the Committee of One Hundred—consciously imitating the political tradition of the Levellers—decided on a policy of direct, non-violent action, organizing a mass sit down outside the Ministry of Defence in Whitehall. The Committee later threatened to do the same in Parliament Square (Taylor and Young 1987). Coming after the Suez debacle in 1956, CND jolted the political establishment's self-confidence and threatened to interfere with its monopoly over defence and foreign policy, which were, even more than penal policy, seen as being well removed from popular scrutiny.

Closer to home concerns, the growth in importance of youth culture, both as a factor in consumer demand and as a de-stabilizing political motif continued to cause anxieties, even resentment. This was exemplified in 1964 by the moral panic that surrounded the activities of the Mods and Rockers. Less clearly working class than the Teds, the Mods and Rockers with their differing and rival dress codes and bikes (or scooters) were initially interpreted as simply disturbing the traditional English seaside bank holiday, but later as representing something far more disruptive, even sinister.

In his carefully observed study of the Mods and Rockers, Cohen (1972) suggests how the older generation, while not wanting a return to the austerity of pre-war Britain, nonetheless felt that young people were probably having things "too good, too soon" and when their sexual freedom was elided with stories in the popular press about drug taking, social discipline was seen to be seriously under threat. Now that National Service had been abandoned, the re-introduction of corporal punishment was seen to be the only "remedy" left. The Mods and Rockers were a sign of things to come. Three years later, in 1966, Britain's first underground paper, *The International Times*, was published in London, and two years after that, rebellious students led by Daniel Cohn Bendit brought France to a standstill. More on this and the counter culture a little later.

Running alongside these extra Parliamentary stresses and strains, and perhaps helping indirectly to reinforce them, was a growing anxiety, particularly from the early 1960s onwards, within more formal political circles that all was not well with the way we did business. At one level this may seem surprising. After all, have I not argued that there was substance in the claim that Britain had "never had it so good"?

Yes, this *was* true, but it was apparently not a matter for unfettered congratulation because while Britain had done well, and indeed continued to do well until 1973, our close neighbours in Europe were doing significantly better. So, for example, between 1950 and 1973 Britain had an average increase in GDP of three per cent, but the same figure for France was 5.1 per cent and for Germany 5.9 per cent (Supple 1994). Furthermore, as the 1960s drew to a close the spectre of unemployment again reared its head; the economic prosperity which had underpinned the broader social and political consensus was seen to be less certain.

This led to a good deal of soul searching, about our exclusion from the European Community, but also and not least, about the nature of the government machine that I outlined in my first essay. Bernard Crick, for example, felt that the Whitehall bureaucracies with their closed network of consultative committees were far too insulated from scrutiny, keeping potentially good ideas out (Crick 1964). This applied as much to the Home Office that made penal policy as it did to the Treasury which steered the economy.

Crick was no revolutionary; he did not believe that we could recreate *polis* of Athens. On the contrary, he wrote as a reformer who believed in strong executive leadership, yet felt that in a modern democracy government should be more open to public scrutiny and to this end he suggested the introduction of Parliamentary Select Committees to call office holders like Home Secretaries, Chancellors and their civil servants to account. He felt the public and their elected representatives had not only the right, but also the duty, to intrude on the cosy, clubbable world of policy making elites. Manoeuvring to exclude the public voice was simply no longer acceptable.

The power of senior civil servants like Newsom and Cunningham at the Home Office was also questioned at this time. They might still control the traffic lights, as Radzinowicz has put it, but did they deserve to? The feeling grew that they represented an Oxbridge dominated, middle class administrative elite who were far more concerned with perpetuating their own power base and promoting "departmental" interests than with promoting effective policies, not least in the face of rising crime rates which implicitly challenged their competence to manage criminal justice policy.

This criticism from within the political establishment and the chattering classes led to the establishment of the Fulton Commission. It was asked to take a fresh look at the Civil Service, in much the way that Northcote and Trevelyan had done a century earlier. Fulton made a number of seminal recommendations about breaching the administrative monopoly of the senior Civil Service which the government pledged to carry through, including the appointment of fixed term outside advisors and the establishment of a Civil Service college where career administrators could receive in-service training to update their skills (HMSO 1968).

The fact that even the metropolitan establishment was attempting to modernize by the mid-1960s was of little interest to those groups who formed the counter culture and took their political briefings from *The International Times, Oz* and *Friendz*. Feeling excluded from the formal democratic system these groups eschewed the formal political apparatus of bourgeois Parliamentary democracy. They looked instead to alternative ways to express their opposition through lifestyles, music, drug taking, alternative theatres and art labs (Nelson 1989). They showed none of the deference towards those in authority that had characterized their parents. Indeed, as Musgrove properly reminds us, the counter culture was itself one of the symptoms of the decline of deference. Neither the traditional authority of status and birth nor the rational norms of the modern bureaucratic state of the expert—and Britain operated a curious mix of both as we have seen—was sufficient to engender consent; authority was rather, "conditional, contractual, on trial" (Musgrove 1974, p 150).

The recognition of this uncertainty came as an enormous shock to those who had enjoyed compliance through their unchallenged control over the burgeoning State network since 1945. John Irwin's characterization of the alienation that was sweeping Europe at this time, fits Britain well. He writes:

> Paralleling the extension of government, there had been a rapid growth in the involvement of major economic organizations with government, forming a vast array of consultative bodies and informal interconnections. At times, this huge corporate network, bureaucratic, faceless and elitist, seemed to be the essential determinate of policy, effectively demoting popular participation and the electoral process. This generated reaction from those organizations and groups excluded from the network, while those within it seemed at times to be demanding the right to set policy even against the government and the electoral will. It was this perception that the state was becoming an unyielding Leviathan concerned primarily with material interests, especially of those groups inside the network, and becoming more remote from the ordinary citizen, which sparked off a wave of protest and alienation in the late 1960s and early 1970s involving interest in new forms of participation in a more de-centralized and "people friendly" system.
>
> (Irwin 1989, p 255)

This alienation spread and took a variety of forms. Direct military action against the State was one solution: the Baader–Meinhof group in Germany, the Red Brigades in Italy. While less destabilizing, the Angry Brigade in Britain were active, placing incendiary devices at the homes of prominent Cabinet Ministers.

There was too a traditional Leninist, or "vanguard", response with the emergence of the International Socialists, later the Socialist Workers Party. However, for the most part in Britain and elsewhere orthodox party politics no longer seemed to be the answer, irrelevant to the process of fundamental change and the need for a permanent political critique.

Radical activists were instead encouraged to work outside of existing political organizations at both national and local levels to develop and build alternative, parallel structures. The final outcome of these interventions was often unknown. Indeed, even to ask about their eventual shape was to invite criticism because it suggested that there was already a preconceived "blueprint" to which all might be expected to conform; this was against the spirit of the journey, too dogmatic, too restrictive. There was no knowing where the articulation of "alternative realities" might lead.

As for the middle aged, conventional party members who looked back with pride to the achievements of postwar governments in securing the Welfare State, particularly Labour governments, they deserved some respect. However, the truth of the matter was that these hard working people were routinely patronized by party leaders who, with the help of trade union leaders, easily out manoeuvred them, dominating party conferences, manipulating "hollow" local parties, and even "fixing" the selection conferences of those wishing to stand for Parliament.

This activist philosophy—*participation* was a precondition for replacing *top down* government by *bottom up* government—led to a whole range of loosely organized, loosely inter-connected groups covering a wide range of policy areas: criminal justice, social security, housing, even the workplace, with the re-birth of the shop stewards' movement. Each of these groups demanded that their previously excluded members be heard, that their experiences be listened to and taken on board by government. After all, the people knew where the shoe pinched, they were the *real* experts. The claim of these *outsider* groups to their own expertise has been noted by Rock:

> Groups of people in the late 1960s and early 1970s, representing themselves as socially and epistemologically oppressed, came to spurn the authority of experts to define and manage their condition and asserted their own existentially-based competence in its place. The professional, they said, did *not* know best. Established knowledge was largely spurious and tyrannical, part of a wider hegemonic control that alienated people from their "species being". Rather than the expert teaching the laity about their condition, it was the laity who should become the instructor. Who could possibly be wiser than the person actually undergoing a debated experience?

> (Rock 1998, p 137)

About this revolt of the client he goes on:

> Those with discontents and problems in the late 1960s and early 1970s turned inwards towards themselves, and others thought to be like themselves for more satisfying classifications, interpretations and solutions. Almost every human group became the focus of its own attendant group: women turned to women … ex-patients to ex-patients … narcotics users to narcotics users … They traded practical knowledge so that Sorbonne students emulated the Berlier workers, prisoners radical students,

psychiatric patients unionized workers ... Often hostile to large bureaucratic organizations, emphasizing the superior experimental understanding of their own members ... recognizing problems dismissed or misinterpreted by others, advocating local initiatives and self improvement, they had widespread political and ideological appeal.

(Rock 1998, p 138)

It is this wider context, the attack on Britain's highly centralized policy making apparatus that I described in *Part I*, that conceptualizes, and gives meaning to, the outsiders' groups whose history I wish to excavate. I start with the prisoners union PROP whose members had for so long had their condition "diagnosed" by either social psychological or medical experts and/or well meaning gentlemen (mostly) penal reformers from the Howard League whose knowledges were then mediated through a myriad of advisory committees and administered by Home Office officials and legitimized by politicians.

It was a time when prisoners attempted to find a collective voice, to make their case in a sustained and systematic way rather than in one-off prison actions or riots.

THE UNION FOR THE PRESERVATION OF THE RIGHTS OF PRISONERS (PROP)

Prison conditions in Britain took a turn for the worse in the late 1960s. This was due to a combination of factors.

First, the number of people held on remand continued to grow, and it was generally agreed that overcrowding among these untried prisoners was particularly hard to justify as many would certainly be found innocent by the courts. Second, pressure on the prison population as a whole was increased by the imposition of longer sentences by the courts, a trend compounded by an increase in the number of *lifers* after the abolition of capital punishment. This had a particular impact on what were known as dispersal prisons, which had been designated to hold all Category A prisoners (following the Mountbatten Report) as an alternative to building a single, Alcatraz-style fortress.

These overcrowding problems were made more intolerable by the ratcheting up of security following Mountbatten. This not only led to the highly visible introduction of things like barbed wire perimeter fencing, guard dogs and the use of more surveillance equipment generally, but was reinforced by a determined POA crackdown on a whole series of established "privileges" for prisoners. Prison officers saw themselves on the ascendancy. Security rather than reform was now the order of the day and prison officers relished the opportunity to show that they were back in charge at the expense of the woolly minded treatment "experts" (Fitzgerald 1977). This new hard line led to growing discontent among prisoners, and where it was accompanied by brutality as at Parkhurst prison in 1969, serious disturbances were reported. For the prisoners at HMP Parkhurst, insult was added to injury when the Gale Report (1969) into what had been the worst prison riot since Dartmoor in 1932 was suppressed, and prisoners punished, even though a leaked copy of the report suggested that complaints of brutality against some staff were supportable (Ryan 1983).

It was against this tense background that a series of prison disturbances were reported early in 1972. During one of these, a peaceful protest among remand prisoners at HMP Brixton, PROP was formally launched from The Prince Arthur, a public house in north London. While PROP had some support from radical academics and other criminal justice professionals, the key players on the executive committee were mostly ex-offenders: people like Dick Pooley, based in Hull, who had spent some 20 years on the inside, and Ted Ward another ex-offender who by that time had been involved in grass roots activity with the Claimants' Union in London.

These people, offenders and ex-offenders like them, were to form the core of the organization. It was their experience that was to count, and while associate membership might be offered to "outside" sympathizers, full membership was only available to prisoners and ex-prisoners. There was a strong feeling, as Mike Fitzgerald was to express it, that the history of prison reform was "filled with the largely futile efforts of middle class liberals to improve the conditions inside prisons, without even consulting with prisoners themselves" (Fitzgerald 1977, p 140). It was time, as Foucault was later to put it rather grandly, that their "subjugated knowledge" was given centre stage (Foucault 1980).

So PROP was not much troubled when Hugh Klare of the Howard League complained in August 1972 that the prisoners' use of the strike weapon was "undemocratic", putting force before "persuasion", "reason" and "compromise" (Fitzgerald 1977, p 160). Prisoners and ex-prisoners were setting the agenda; policy and tactics were now being driven from below, from HMP Brixton and The Prince Arthur and not from Whitehall and the Athenaeum. What could be more democratic than this?

One should add here, and it is no small matter, that local branches of the POA were also flexing their muscles at this time, increasingly operating quite independently from their National Executive which, like many other unions at the time, was unable to control its rank and file and deliver agreements reached with the Prison Department civil servants in Whitehall. In the face of these local pressures (from both sides) the Home Office was arguably less firmly in control of the prison system in the 1970s than at any time since its nationalization in 1877. (For more on the state of prisons in the 1970s, see Fitzgerald and Sim 1979.)

The Prisoners' Charter

The right to represent prisoners was at the core of PROP's original charter. This demanded that all prisoners should be allowed to become PROP members, that PROP representatives be openly and fairly elected and, where appropriate, that these should serve on relevant prison committees with prison officers and prison governors. In short, PROP wanted the right to operate as if it was a trade union representing its members at the local level. As for national level, PROP should negotiate on prison issues, including on issues such as pay, with the Home Office. After all, on this issue, and on other bread and butter issues, it was PROP's members and not the Howard League's members who really understood what prisoners wanted.

In order to facilitate this activity, PROP called for an end to the blanket application of the Official Secrets Act to just about all prison business, and the end to the practice of censorship, not least when this involved interfering with correspondence between prisoners and their legal representatives. Allied to this were demands for the right to take legal action against the Home Office and for prisoners to have legal representation at disciplinary hearings of the Boards of Visitors such as those which had been responsible for handing out tough sentences to prisoners at HMP Durham (1963) and HMP Parkhurst (1969). There was also the demand for legal help in applying for parole which had been introduced in the Criminal Justice Act 1967, and for far greater transparency in the whole parole process, such as the board giving reasons for its refusal in an individual case.

Wider civil rights issues, like the right of prisoners to have doctors of their own choosing, their right to marriage and their right to take part in local and national elections, were also included, as was a package of demands to help prisoners on their release. This went beyond the call for prisoners to be credited with national insurance stamps, to include the demand that criminal records be destroyed after a given period, that an ex-prisoner's slate might be wiped clean.

The sheer audacity of these demands, which were underpinned by a call for greater public accountability of the operation of the Prison Service, took the media by surprise and sustained its interest. Here was something more than a one-off complaint by "old lags" about prison food; more even, than an isolated, violent protest against the brutalities of prison life, stories of which had begun to surface in the media during that time; rather it was a wide ranging and highly articulate critique of a major social institution whose largely unaccountable operations had been obscured from public view for more than a century, of concern to no one much except a small body of well meaning prison reformers whose honest efforts I outlined in my first essay.

While PROP's charter of rights was acknowledged by many critics of the prison system as a reasonably authentic reflection of prisoners' grievances at the time—even the Howard League did not quarrel too much with this — the idea that prisoners might have a say through their own trade union was never accepted by the Home Office. Dick Pooley wrote to the Home Secretary who ignored him. Home Office officials were advised to do likewise, and PROP literature was confiscated in many prisons.

The Prison Officers' Association was affronted by PROP's very existence. Most of its members thought it a threat to good order and security in prisons and they made these views known to government. It is true, as Fitzgerald rightly reminds us, that by July 1972 the Home Office was anxious about the situation in prisons and he called governors together urging that improvements be made (Fitzgerald 1977, p 150). However, the Home Secretary, aware of increasing hostility from local POA branches, again refused to acknowledge PROP which then called for a national sit down strike by prisoners for early August 1972.

The strike had a sizeable impact, with thousands of prisoners across Britain taking part, even though the Home Office tried to deny it. It is probably true that many of the prisoners taking part in these peaceful demonstrations had only a limited or garbled view of what PROP stood for, but this did not dampen their support, and the nationwide success of the protest was impressive given the traditional barriers to communication between prisons and the outside world. Without the high level of media interest the protest would have failed; it was the media which spread the news about the planned strike across the land rather than PROP.

This was the high point of PROP's visibility. The movement's capacity to mobilize and speak collectively for prisoners declined rapidly after this protest, and though there were bitter skirmishes with the POA at local prisons such as HMPs Albany and Gartree around this time, PROP faded away as a cohesive national union. Few tangible gains were secured by the strike and prisoners quickly seemed to lose interest in the potential of PROP as a regular trade union. The Home Office appeared to have weathered the storm. Britain might be edging its way towards a more participative democracy, but this was not going to extend to a prisoners' union for a long while yet.

I will touch on the reasons for this failure shortly, but in the meantime it is important to remember that PROP remained very active as a pressure group, if not as a trade union *per se*, interpreting the world from the prisoner's point of view and helping to achieve some notable victories during the 1970s, some of which have had lasting repercussions.

PROP in the penal lobby

These successes are worth recalling. For example, PROP took an uncompromising lead in the fight against control units. These units were introduced at Wakefield prison in 1973/4 to cope with what were taken to be a hard core of difficult offenders in British prisons. The plan was to isolate these "trouble makers" from the mainstream of the prison population and then subject them to a very strict regime, with long periods of isolation, over a period of 180 days. The Control Units Action Group (1974), in which PROP participated, was eventually successful in forcing the Home Secretary to close these units.

A few years later, it was PROP that broke the news about the use of MUFTI (Minimum Use of Force Tactical Intervention) squads in British prisons. In August 1979 a number of prisoners in the maximum security wing at HMP Wormwood Scrubs were holding a peaceful protest about the withdrawal of some of their privileges when a MUFTI squad ran out of control wielding long staves and pickaxe handles. A number of prisoners were injured in the fighting, and many more were disciplined as a result of the assault. PROP not only prised the truth out of a reluctant Prison Department about what had really happened on that night—its officials had been less than forthcoming—it also brought to light, *en passant*, the existence of the specially trained MUFTI squads which had never been justified or debated in Parliament nor the rules governing their use published (*Abolitionist*, No. 11 1982).

PROP also criticized the Prison Department over its handling of the Hull prison riots in 1976. HMP Hull was a dispersal prison, and its Board of Visitors had warned the Home Office of tensions there, but they were ignored. The first Hull riot occurred after it was alleged that a prisoner had been badly assaulted by prison officers in the segregation unit. When requests to visit this prisoner were refused, other prisoners rioted. This lasted for nearly four days, and when the prison was re-taken one wing was pretty well unusable. Jake Prescott, a member of the Angry Brigade, was in Hull at this time (PROP 1977).

The bald facts of this riot are not seriously disputed. What is at issue was the second riot which happened when prison officers ran amok, seriously ill treating prisoners on their "surrender". Following a Home Office inquiry which concluded that no serious assaults had taken place PROP launched its own quasi-judicial, public inquiry in May 1977. As a result of this inquiry, and the extensive police investigations that followed it, eight prison officers were eventually found guilty of assault in the courts.

This result did not come early enough to influence the Hull Board of Visitors which handed out very harsh punishments to those involved in the riots. One prisoner lost 720 days' remission. The manner in which these boards conducted their business was controversial. The prisoner's right to call witnesses was circumscribed and there was no right to legal representation or appeal, except on procedural grounds. It was the unfairness of these procedures that led PROP to support one of the Hull prisoners in appealing against his punishment, and when the case finally reached the Lords of Appeal in 1979 *(St German)* it was held that boards *were* accountable to the courts in the exercise of their disciplinary function.

The significance of this decision, and PROP's role in providing the platform to secure it, should not be underestimated. Previously, with the exception of Sydney Gilder's success at the European Court of Human Rights which had secured the right to privacy in correspondence between a prisoners and his solicitor *(Gilder,* ECHR 1975), the courts had taken a hands off view towards the administration of prisons. In rulings such as *Argon* v. *Anderson* (Lord Goddard, 1943) and *Becker* v. *Home Office* (Lord Denning, 1972) British judges had allowed prison governors and Boards of Visitors to do more or less as they pleased (Owen and Livingston 1993). Their Lordships had adopted the extreme position that even where it could be proved that a governor had disobeyed the prison rules this did not necessarily give cause for action. If it were otherwise, they argued, then the prison governor's life would be made intolerable. He or she would always be fearful of legal action, and prison discipline would surely suffer as a consequence. Prisons were dark places, and the courts should support those who ran them, even when the rules had been bent or broken.

This attitude meant that prisoners had no effective redress before the courts. The day-to-day administration of the prison system, which was for all intents and purposes politically unaccountable, and shielded from wider public scrutiny by the blanket application of the Official Secrets Act, was also legally unaccountable. The *St German* judgement was a landmark in helping to change this.

It is important to acknowledge that there had been a more general growth in the application of judicial review across a whole range of government activities, that the courts had begun to intervene and question how government departments applied statute law (and regulations) to a degree that was unthinkable in the 1950s and 1960s when the great departments of State ruled unchallenged. So PROP's contribution has to be seen in this wider context. On the other hand, the case had to be made in the prison sector, and in many ways it was the outcome of more than a decade of sustained, radical agitation around this issue. For example, the prison rules that Goddard and Denning were so determined to place beyond the reach of judicial review were mostly unknown to many prisoners, who lived in a Kafka-like environment unsure whether or not they were abusing them.

The system basically worked—and to a degree still does—like this. The legislative framework governing prisons at this time was laid down by an Act of Parliament: the Prison Act 1952. Like most primary legislation this was widely drawn. So in order to give more general guidance on how this Act was to be interpreted and implemented, the Prison Department published its own prison rules that were sent to every governor. These rules, in turn, were then modified by a steady stream of Circulars and Instructions. All very reasonable, you might think. The problem is that most of this material was shielded from prisoners and attempts to publicize it were circumscribed by the threat of the Official Secrets Act. With PROP's encouragement and the support of a number of other lobby groups and academics who called the government's bluff on the Official Secrets Act (Cohen and Taylor 1976) this material did reach prisoners who, albeit slowly, got a better purchase on their rights in the 1970s and 1980s. But it was a slow process that the Home Office fought against every step of the way (Owen and Livingston 1993).

All this activity suggests a sustained challenge to the authority of metropolitan administrative, political and liberal elites to dictate prisoners' priorities. This challenge, across a wide range of issues, was carried on well into the 1980s. Those at the hard end of the penal apparatus mobilized and declared their own agenda. For example, prisoners took to the public their "client" views about "solitary" (control and containment), about the growing use of the "liquid cosh" (drug therapy) and, as an integral part of that process, opened up the closed world of the prison to wider public scrutiny and "alternative realities" which were sharply at odds with official, expert discourse. PROP might not have secured a place at the negotiating table as a recognized trade union, its goal in 1972, but its outsider influence was nonetheless real and tangible in the ways I have described.

The experience of imprisonment was not transformed by its efforts, but it was made more visible, and to a degree, more contestable. One of the problems in 1972, according to Fitzgerald, had been that the outside help necessary to sustain PROP as an effective trade union was not forthcoming. There was he writes, insufficient

> backing from other academics and others involved in the penal system. Although PROP had originally announced its intentions to the National Deviancy Conference [NDC] in York some weeks before it was publicly identified, there was only a limited, positive response to its calls for help. The NDC is an organization for radical criminologists and others, presenting an alternative voice to that of the Home Office and its satellites (particularly in Cambridge). The group had tried to forge links between theory and praxis, and to this end has provided a forum plus financial help for many groups, including representatives for the gay, women's and mental patients', and prisoners' movements. However, the success of the NDC in linking theory to practice is extremely limited. In the case of the prisoners' union, perhaps most of the delegates supported the ideas it embodied, but only a handful were later to be personally involved. These few provided platforms from which the PROP organizers tried to rally support ... For the large majority of NDC members, however, this involvement with PROP has to be seen as part of their generalized romantic flirtation with the counter culture of the 1960s and its off- shoots in the early 1970s.

(Fitzgerald 1977, pp 186/187)

If attracting outside support was difficult, trying to educate and politicize inside support was even more of a problem. Fitzgerald elsewhere suggests that:

> Although members of such groups as the Angry Brigade have had an undoubted influence inside, we should be careful of exaggerating it. In Britain, the whole issue of possible politicization has hardly been discussed. It is crucial to recognize, therefore, that almost all the prisoners involved in demonstrations of the summer of 1972 were motivated by the conditions in which they were forced to exist rather than because of some wider understanding of the importance of imprisonment in advanced, capitalist societies.
>
> (Fitzgerald 1977, pp 181/182)

These quotations suggest the involvement in the prisoners' movement of a politics that went well beyond the narrow strategic concerns of PROP to secure prison reform. For example, what was meant by complaining that prisoners were *only* motivated by a desire to improve prison conditions? What else should they be motivated by? And what exactly was meant by an alternative voice to the Home Office and its satellites if it did not mean the voice of rank and file prisoners?

I want to address these important questions through a brief discussion of the role of the National Deviancy Conference. This will help to explain how *forms of radical politics came to be inscribed on the issue of penal reform* from the late 1960s, an inscription which suggests a more complex and divided society than the consensual one I outlined in my first essay.

THE NATIONAL DEVIANCY CONFERENCE

The National Deviancy Conference (NDC) flashed like a meteor across the intellectual firmament of the late 1960s, illuminating almost every aspect of the study of crime and deviance in Britain, until it waned in the mid-1980s before finally disappearing with the rise of the New Right. It took on the academic criminological establishment, which at the time it explicitly identified with the government sponsored Cambridge Institute of Criminology led by Leon Radzinowicz and the London based Institute for the Study and Treatment of Delinquency.[1] It did this in a number of ways and on various sites, sometimes directly, sometimes indirectly.

First, and foremost, by focusing on sociological approaches to the study of deviancy the NDC challenged the prevailing orthodoxies around law and psychiatry which tended to take official definitions of crime and the criminal for granted, failing to acknowledge that crime and the criminal are social constructs, the outcome of sometimes complex social and political processes and interactions. This approach was not only bad academic practice—no self-respecting academic takes the object of his or her study for granted—it also came close to turning criminology into an uncritical tool of government which was in business, not to generate appreciative studies of the social construction of crime and deviance, but rather to look for practical solutions to deal with those whose behaviour Parliament had defined as criminal.

---

[1] Now the Centre for Crime and Justice Studies.

Cohen expressed and refined this trenchant academic critique—with its implicit political message—in 1974 when he observed that:

the correctional stance takes for granted the objective of getting rid of the deviant phenomenon under question—and in doing so it "systematically interferes with the capacity to empathize and thus understand the subject of inquiry" ... Mainstream criminology has refused to go beyond the correctional stance: a weak demand from sociologists is to question the applicability of this ideology; a stronger demand would be to accept appreciation and the subjective view is the only defensible one.

(Cohen 1974, pp 4/5)

He went on:

The major institutions of British criminology have apparently quite unselfconsciously accepted the goals of social control, taking up, within these, various correctional or reformative stances. Contributions are made by those ... who are sponsored by the system (e.g. doing research financed by the Home Office) or by the numerous institutions whose policy is to encourage co-operation between the so-called "scientific" and the so-called "practical" objectives."

(Cohen 1974, pp 16/17)

The sociological approaches which informed this challenge to the role of British criminology were not accorded much credibility by the Home Office (Faulkner 2000), while they simply irritated academic grandees like Sir Leon Radzinowicz who was later to accuse the founders of the NDC of having behaved like "naughty schoolboys" (Radzinowicz 2000). For others though, particularly those ambitious, young, academic social scientists and social workers/probation officers who attended the NDC in the late 1960s and 1970s, they had a strong political resonance (For more on the academic background to the "new criminology," see Taylor I, Walton P and Young J 1974.)

Many of these young participants had quite different political histories— some were Anarchists who had been active in CND and the Committee of 100, others drifted in from the International Socialists with a Leninist perspective, others still came in from the Labour Party. However there was a general disillusionment with conventional politics and the "usual channels" and a determination instead to secure change from outside of the formal political (and bureaucratic) structures by giving active support to a range of groups, including many client-led groups, across the welfare and criminal justice systems. It was this that led the NDC to give support to organizations such as PROP, CaseCon and Radical Alternatives to Prison (RAP). The NDC was thus allied to the politics of the counter culture, a reflection which perhaps helps to explain why it could never be resurrected in the 1980s in spite of a nostalgic desire to do so. The moment had gone.

It is obvious that the level of support offered by the NDC was insufficient to sustain groups like PROP and CaseCon, as their histories testify. This may, or may not, be construed as a criticism of the NDC, however, my main concern here is to stress that the intellectual and political critique around the Conference— though it was not *entirely* responsible for generating this critique—opened up a debate about the penal system that went beyond the narrow reform agenda of traditional groups like the Howard League, or PROP for that matter. It located the penal system firmly in other social processes, processes which inevitably reflected material and other inequalities—gender inequalities for example—which fed into the social construction and control of crime and deviancy. Thus, when Mike Fitzgerald spoke about the function of prisons in advanced capitalist societies *both* Dick Pooley and Hugh Klare were being asked to look at the penal system in an entirely new light, to inscribe on their limited struggle for change, a more critical, political perspective.

To illustrate this shift, and the strategic dilemmas it imposed, I now intend to excavate the place of Radical Alternatives to Prison (RAP), an organization whose origins lie outside of the academic tradition I have just outlined, but whose critique owed much to it.

RADICAL ALTERNATIVES TO PRISON (RAP)

Radical Alternatives to Prison was established in 1970, taking over the slender assets of the Prison Medical Reform Council. The Council had been established in 1943 to monitor the treatment of conscientious objectors, and while it had attracted new support as a result of the imprisonment of some members of the Committee of 100, it was all but moribund by the late 1960s. With additional financial support from Canon John Collins, a fervent CND supporter with radical political credentials, RAP brought a wholly new style of politics to the penal lobby.

In the first place, RAP was very different in terms of both membership and style from other lobby groups. Rather than being run by a formally elected executive committee of the great and the good as was the Howard League, RAP's open Nucleus working out of east London was made up of younger, sixties-trained social workers, probation officers, student lawyers and locally based political activists, some of them working class. At lobby meetings the informal appearance of its members marked it out from the suited respectability of the established lobby. So too did its style of operating.

Sometimes with experience of university sit-ins, or other forms of direct, community action, RAP's members were altogether less deferential to authority figures such as home secretaries and prison governors. They took some delight in making sharp, critical interventions—often in tandem with PROP—at these meetings, or mounting well publicized demonstrations outside prisons like HMP Wandsworth or HMP Holloway. Neither RAP nor PROP was in the least worried if such interventions embarrassed officials. After all, were these people not supposed to be our representatives and servants rather than our masters? (I recall some members of the established lobby feeling uncomfortable with these strident, sometimes emotionally very powerful, interventions.)

But RAP was different in terms of substance as well as style from groups like the Howard League and the revamped umbrella group of prisoners' aid societies, the National Association for the Care and Resettlement of Offenders (NACRO). To begin with, and crucially, RAP did not believe in prison reform. This agenda had played itself out. Prisons might re-cycle delinquents, and the government's own figures on re-conviction rates confirmed that prisons were very successful in this respect, but the one thing they did not do was to reform offenders. RAP therefore took an abolitionist perspective. Alternatives to custody should be developed instead, with prisons being eventually phased out altogether. These alternatives should preferably be locally based and informally driven and, arguably, would have a better chance of reforming, especially if they were left in the hands of ordinary folk rather than entrusted to experts or professionals.

This radical position reflected wider, critical perspectives that were developing, especially in The Netherlands and Scandinavia, about the criminal justice system generally, and not just prisons. Briefly put, what lay behind these perspectives was the view that somewhere during the process of industrialization, civil law and criminal law had parted company. As a result, settling many important disputes had now been entrusted to the State in the form of the criminal justice system: a vast, impersonal, centralized, bureaucratic machine which was detached from local communities, and which often acted in ways which were against the interests of both the offender and the victim. It was a machine designed to deliver pain rather than to secure justice. Abolishing the modern criminal justice system was therefore a pre-requisite to returning the resolution of disputes back to "ordinary people" and away from the criminal justice professionals (Christie 1982).

To say that RAP's thinking reflected these perspectives is not to say that it embraced them all. Indeed, British abolitionism was always less full blown than its continental European counterparts, more aware perhaps that, so boldly stated, it leaves a lot of very awkward questions unanswered about social control in large complex societies. On the other hand, by echoing these perspectives, by highlighting the persistent failure of the modern prison and calling for its abolition RAP's message was a dramatic (and strident) challenge to the Howard League and quangos like NACRO whose *raison d'être* was prison reform, and whose very *modus operandi* as experts was co-terminous with the highly centralized, modern State.

If such a critique unsettled the Howard League, and there is evidence that it did eventually force it to jettison its belief in the potential of the prisons to reform, there were other criticisms to follow that made the League feel even more uncomfortable. These centred on the notion that the penal system was operated in the interests of the powerful; that it disciplined the less privileged while turning a blind eye to those with wealth and power. Take, for example, this extract from RAP's pamphlet on the new "therapeutic" Holloway prison for women against which it campaigned vigorously:

> Underlying the plans for the new Holloway ... is the unquestioned acceptance of the whole superstructure of the law, the courts, the police, the definitions of who is the "criminal", in a word "justice". The whole process of labelling a person as criminal, of which prison is a small but important part, is taken for granted. It is very important to see that the definition of certain sorts of acquisitiveness and violence as "criminal" and the acceptance of other sorts of acquisitiveness and violence as commendable, reflects and perpetuates the vested interest and inequalities of power, wealth and status that have characterized British society ... through powerful landowners and ruthless industrialists to today. The law, its substance and its application, are rooted in the inequalities of the past. Thus the law has been compared to a cobweb—it lets the big bumble bee through and catches the small insect ...

(RAP 1972, p 12)

This curious admixture of primitive labelling theory and Marxism—explicit class analysis can be found elsewhere in RAP literature—added yet another dimension to RAP's critique of the established penal lobby, suggesting again that the business of penal politics could not be abstracted from wider social and political processes with their attendant inequalities. Furthermore, while the political education required to make similar connections had been a struggle for those involved with PROP in 1972, there were plenty in RAP—though certainly not all—who were all too receptive to the critiques which echoed the NDC, even if they articulated them somewhat crudely.

The challenge these critiques presented to the established penal lobby was deeply resented, not least by the liberal establishment. Members of the Howard League, NACRO, members of the government's Advisory Council on the Penal System and, no doubt, many penal operatives in the field saw themselves as the nation's conscience on these issues. It was people like themselves who had quietly and discreetly—and often across party political lines—pushed the spirit of "welfare" in the 1940s and then manned the barricades against the "hangers and the floggers" over corporal and capital punishment in the 1950s and 1960s. It was surely such people, later to be derided by a Labour Home Secretary as "Hampstead liberals", who had stemmed the tide against England's punitive obsession, or that at least is how they saw it. (Hampstead in north-west London is identified as the home of the liberal, professional classes, but this should not be taken too literally.) Yet, now they were being told, not only that their *raison d'être* of penal reform was a chimera, but that penal policy was connected by a strong thread to the politics of oppression. This was a connection that few of them made, or even worse, had ever admitted.

An article in the *Prison Service Journal* expressed resentment at these attempts to "politicize" and "radicalize" penal reform. An anonymous contributor who had been at the launch of RAP's Holloway pamphlet observed:

> I came away with the slight but uncomfortable feeling that people's goodwill and integrity is being used for other purposes besides that of penal reform. I believe profoundly that crime and punishment must be kept out of the political arena. It is far too emotive and emotional an area to allow it to be used for political ends.

(Prison Service Journal, New Series, No. 8, October 1972, p 8)

It was just such analytical naiveté that RAP sought to confront. It was always likely, however, that the Prison Service would be far less exposed to such dangerous radicalism than some other parts of the penal apparatus. Nowhere was this more evident than in the Probation Service where a very radical form of politics took root in the early 1970s through an action group, NMAG, whose agenda closely reflected RAP's programme, to the consternation of some Home Office officials.

NAPO MEMBERS' ACTION GROUP (NMAG)

Although the politics of this action group, formed in 1972, were explicitly Marxist, it was essentially a loose, non-sectarian socialist alliance which attracted between 100 and 150 young, main grade officers who were committed to the Probation Service, but determined to change it from within (*Abolitionist*, No. 9 1981). It produced a magazine three times a year called *Probe* and operated as a federation of local groups linked by a national coordinating committee, so in the spirit of the times, it was driven from below. At the outset it was more concerned with issues of pay and democratization, but as a result of its contacts with RAP and PROP it soon developed a broader agenda which was pretty much compatible, if not always identical, with those groups.

So, for example, NMAG supported PROP's *Charter of Rights*, wanted to reform the Official Secrets Act, called for the immediate lifting of prison censorship and demanded the abolition of Boards of Visitors. It also called for the abolition of parole. The argument here was that if prisons did not reform offenders there was no point in pretending that at some stage they would reach a peak in their training and therefore be safe for release, albeit on licence. It also supported RAP in its campaign to close prisons and to put pressure on magistrates and judges to find alternatives to custody wherever possible. It specifically identified crime as a product of an aggressive, acquisitive and exploitative individualism associated with advanced western capitalist societies (*Abolitionist*, No. 9 1981).

NMAG probably had an influence out of all proportion to its membership as when, for example, it captured the moral high ground in the fierce debate surrounding the publication of the Younger Report (1974) whose recommendations would have given probation officers a far more controlling function over young adult offenders. It would, for example, have allowed probation officers to apply to the courts for the temporary detention of their clients for up to 72 hours. While it is true that NMAG's influence genuinely reflected the Probation Service's ambivalence about the new role being suggested for it, this anxiety was skilfully worked upon by NMAG activists at NAPO conferences and a variety of *ad hoc* meetings around the country (Ryan 1978).

The extent of this rank and file activity was communicated to the Home Office; it was reported that:

Last year's [NAPO] report referred to pressure groups appearing in the Association for the first time. These groups have swiftly extended their influence and the Conference in 1973 largely responded to their eloquence and careful organization. The constitutional amendments were aimed at giving more power to the ordinary members (especially the main grade officers) and lessening of the authority of the NEC. The great increase in the number of motions reflected a similar point of view: those who proposed them believing that as many decisions as possible should be made by General Meetings.

(Quoted in King and Jarvis 1977, p 84)

Those who ran the Probation Service were quite unnerved by this. Suddenly reliable, main grade probation officers, often ex-army, wearing grey flannel trousers and sober sports coats, the sort of people who could be relied upon to behave sensibly in court and firmly towards clients, were being replaced by people in jeans, straight out of university: people who had been trained to *theorize* about social work practices, who were more hostile to the courts than to their clients, and who sought to mobilize wider, political alliances outside the service with radical intent. As a *Probe* editorial was to confirm:

> We must escape from the easy view of probation as an elite section of the social services, dealing with people different from the rest of us, distinguished by their criminality—people who can be brought to terms with society by casework, kindness and our expertise. When considered as part of an unjust social and economic system, our clients become catalysts for our involvement in political, trade union activity, in cooperation with them and with other workers.
>
> (Quoted in King and Jarvis 1977, p 84)

The dangers this posed were clear to academics, the Home Office and the judiciary when they met at the Cambridge Institute of Criminology in 1976 to debate penal policy making in England. The indirect control the Home Office had traditionally exerted over the shape and direction of the service was being contested, and chief probation officers could no longer be relied upon to bring the rank and file into line with government thinking. True, the gap between rank and file and chief officers was partly due to the rapid growth in the service and the introduction of more managerial grades, but it was openly acknowledged that the nature of the divide was more ideological than managerial. Delegates were told to wake up to the fact that some of these radical leaders were "frankly Marxist", and that these "Marxist entrepreneurs" were out to subvert an innocent, "democratic" and "well intentioned organization"(quoted in King and Jarvis 1977, p 86).

Not all those present at the Cambridge conference were quite so dismissive or felt quite so threatened, and NMAG never got anywhere near to "subverting" the service, if that had ever been its intention. On the other hand, what the Cambridge discussion clearly acknowledged was the existence of an influential and radical critique which was threatening to change the service. What had once been a deferential, evangelical profession owing its origins to the work of the church court missionaries, and then updated into individual "case workers" in the 1950s, was now being encouraged to engage with a constellation of groups like RAP and PROP whose posture was anything but deferential, and whose agenda was driven by a political radicalism which addressed structural problems and not individual weakness. It is no wonder that NAPO's hierarchy moved to exclude groups like RAP and PROP (Ryan 1978).

Posturing nihilism?

For those who were beginning to look outside the criminal justice system to understand the complex material and social processes involved in the production of deviant or criminal behaviour, and who saw the penal apparatus as being largely oppressive, working for change within the existing system presented some real and complex strategic dilemmas. How, for example, were they to approach the introduction of community service orders?

These orders had been provided for by a Conservative government in the Criminal Justice Act 1972. They were intended as an alternative to a prison sentence. The idea was that judges would be allowed to sentence offenders for up to 240 hours of community service instead of sending them to prison. What tasks they would be ordered to carry out would vary, depending on the requirements identified by local voluntary associations. They might, for example, be required to help redecorate an old people's home, or help to build an adventure playground in some inner-city housing estate. It was seen as a way of making offenders put something back into the community which, by their criminal actions, they had damaged, and who knows, the experience of helping the less fortunate and the vulnerable might even reform them.

RAP might have been expected to have endorsed this provision. But it did not. Instead, it urged it members to be cautious, arguing that:

> Prisons have long since lost any pretensions of leading their inmates towards a good and useful life and have stood for the past century as stark symbols of social control and repression. It must not be forgotten that alternative schemes produced within the existing framework of society must necessarily have the same function ... the violence and coercion of prison speaks for itself ... it is not so with community service— seduction has always been the liberal reformers' weapon.
>
> The values of community service are bourgeois; the task that people will be asked to undertake will reinforce these values. In such action there is no real service to the community.
>
> To put it another way, if you work in the Home Office, then clearly it is in your interest to utilize community service to its maximum—it will be more effective than your prisons, attract significantly less criticism. But if you accept a radical critique of society, if you believe it is fundamentally characterized by conflict, ridden with class divisions and dominance you should treat community service with more care and subdue your liberal instincts ... Beware Greeks bearing gifts.
>
> (*RAP Newsletter*, March 1975)

It was just this sort of posturing nihilism, *as they saw it*, that so infuriated liberals, and I would have to have admit there was some unhelpful *a priori* reasoning in *some* of RAP's literature which implied a determination not to engage with the criminal justice system on any terms (Ryan and Ward 1992). On the other hand, such liberal impatience was by no means entirely justified. For example, RAP's position that community orders would only secure a positive outcome for offenders if they were entered into voluntarily has much to commend it. Furthermore, its concern that such orders would all too quickly become used, not as a genuine alternative to prison, but instead in place of other, lesser sentences, such as the fine, so widening the net of formal social control, was soon shown to be true by the Home Office's *own* research.[2]

So with the critical help of academic activists like Cohen and Mathiesen, RAP did try to think through the complex problems of engaging with the system, and in its Newham Alternative Project tried to resolve them by operating, with the permission of the Crown Court and with a little help from probation officers, the deferred sentence which had also been included in the Criminal Justice Act 1972 as section 22. What this did was to allow judges to defer passing a prison or other sentence if they had reason to believe that the offender's circumstances were about to take a "turn for the better". He or she might, for example, have been offered work or permanent accommodation. The Newham Alternative Project

---

[2] For more on the origins and development of community service, see Scott D and Whitfield D (1993), *Paying Back: Twenty Years of Community Service* (Winchester: Waterside Press).

sought to persuade judges and offenders that they could play a decisive role in securing that "turn for the better," and with the help of local community volunteers did succeed in getting a number of offenders referred to it from the Snaresbrook Crown Court (Dronfield 1980).[3] Local magistrates had refused to cooperate.

RAP also engaged, as we have seen, with arguments around the day-to-day operation of the prison system, though this too was something that its members had to think through. After all, if RAP was genuinely committed to prison abolition embracing prison *reform* might seem odd, and certainly many of its members were cool towards the idea. However, most of its more active members, some of them directly influenced by the work of the Norwegian abolitionist Thomas Mathiesen, came to support the notion that some reforms were acceptable.

Mathiesen drew a distinction between negative and positive reforms. For example, a negative reform, and one which RAP was happy to support, was the demand to end the censorship of prisoners' mail. Censorship was one of many official mechanisms used to secure the isolation of the prison, to hide its brutal realities from the public. To get rid of censorship would therefore hasten the end of the prison system. A positive reform on the other hand, would be one that supported the use of more psychotherapists and new treatment paradigms which would simply further strengthen the myth that prison works (Mathiesen 1974).

This distinction enabled RAP to work closely with a group like PROP, which was always more attracted to "bread and butter" issues outlined in its charter than abolition, and even groups like the Howard League and the newly emerging Prison Reform Trust which were simply in place to make prisons "work"—and last. It also made working with the Probation Service a continuing strategic possibility, though NAPO sought to undermine NMAG after a particularly bruising national conference at Weymouth in 1974.

Of course, it is easy to understand why some observers sometimes felt that RAP offered "not a single constructive idea" (Ryan 1978, p 132), deliberately choosing to attack this or that penal practice (imprisoning people for the non-payment of fines, for example) without explaining what punishment to put in its place. It is also true that RAP's interventions were not always as sound or as well researched as they might have been, and there was a degree of romanticism about some of its experiments and a failure to face up to their shortcomings. On the other hand, to have suggested that RAP offered nothing constructive or self-critical was not only demonstrably untrue (Box Grainger 1983; Cohen 1979; Ward 1984), it also underestimated the strategic complexities and practical limits, including financial ones, which faced those who sought to challenge penal orthodoxies, even at a time when official confidence in those orthodoxies was faltering. Mathiesen spoke about these dilemmas:

> The opponent of the prevailing order is therefore presented with the choice between specifying alternatives—and thereby becoming very close to the prevailing order in

---

[3] Cohen attended RAP's Nucleus in the late 1970s and wrote a critical, strategic introduction to Dronfield's (1980) study of the Newham Alternative Project. Laurie Taylor also helped by scripting a RAP community television programme.

what he suggests—or emphasizing completely different values—and thereby being rejected as irresponsible and unrealistic.

(Mathiesen 1974, p 113)

Seen in this light, RAP's failure to engage fully and its eventual collapse in the early 1980s is perhaps more understandable. However, there is evidence that RAP evolved and refined its critique and its tactics, benefiting directly from, among other sources, the rise of the feminist movement.

WOMEN IN PRISON (WIP)

Pat Carlen has done well to remind us that it was not until well into the 1970s that traditional views about women's criminality were confronted and displaced, and any serious critical attempt was made to understand their lawbreaking and criminalization in the context of the other "concealed" and more complex forms of oppression which women endure (Carlen 1985, p 6). This lack of a genuinely critical interest in women and crime was reflected in the re-building of the old Holloway prison in north London in the 1960s as a "secure hospital" to give "the impression of normality" where "treatment" was to be administered to the "sick". RAP had challenged this official obfuscation and campaigned against the new Holloway as a *prison* with some energy in 1972, pointing out, among other things, that such tight security was simply inappropriate for most women offenders.

However, in spite of this robust intervention and the polite concern of other reform groups like the Howard League, it was not until Women in Prison was founded in 1983 that women prisoners got their own voice and made their own demands. WIP was founded in 1982 by an ex-prisoner, Chris Tchaikovsky, who had been asked to prepare a report on prisons for the Women's Committee of the Greater London Council (GLC). As a direct result of this work came the idea of a support group for women prisoners. The idea was to offer practical help to women in HMP Holloway and to campaign on wider issues of policy. The GLC was persuaded that this was within its terms of reference and provided funds for workers. (The local authority, the London Borough of Islington also gave financial support.)

WIP adopted a two-track strategy when campaigning. First, it identified a number of issues that were common to all prisoners, whatever their gender or race. So, it was in favour of abolishing the Official Secrets Act, the ending of mail censorship, the replacement of parole, legal representation on any internal disciplinary hearings and so forth, demands which, broadly speaking, many of the new and more radical groups in the lobby such as PROP and RAP were happy to go along with. However, it obviously campaigned around issues that were particularly of interest to women, and therefore called for an end to the "punitive" disciplinary code for women and more appropriate welfare and training provision, as well as an end to the discriminatory sentencing practices which often, and quite unnecessarily and unjustly, swept many women into prisons like Holloway in the first place (*The Abolitionist*, No. 15, 1983).

Again in the spirit of the times, most of WIP's active members were ex-prisoners. Only they could overcome their own "invisibility" and "tell it how it was". Some women academics lent their support it is true, and some men were accepted for "funding purposes" but the main campaigning work was mostly done by women ex-prisoners. In pursuit of this strategy one of the things WIP did most successfully was to give space to personal testimony, so slowly but surely what was happening to women in HMP Durham's H wing and then later in HMP Holloway's C1 wing became apparent and the official discourse of "treatment" was decoded. In short, having "been largely ignored by prison campaigners, prison visitors and by officials in the penal system" women prisoners now had a critical, campaigning voice (*The Abolitionist,* No. 15, 1983).

It is also worth registering here, however, that apart from campaigning about prisons *per se*, WIP published a number of interesting fragments exploring the complexities of women's oppression and how these were reflected in (and through) the criminal justice system. These discussions were never easy, reflecting perhaps Pat Carlen's observation that "the essential woman criminal does not exist" (Carlen 1985, p 10). This was a fairly prudent position to have adopted during the early 1980s when fractures were beginning to develop in the feminist movement, divisions which were reflected in the penal lobby itself where distinct and separate pressure groups for black and Asian women prisoners began to emerge in the 1980s.

WIP worked in tandem with other lobby groups reasonably successfully at this time. For example, with another GLC sponsored group, INQUEST, which investigated deaths in State custody since 1981, it pursued a number of inquiries into prison deaths such as those of Janet Smith and Mavis Jones at HMP Holloway and HMP Buckley Hall respectively. Its relationship with PROP was accommodating, provided that the latter kept its distance. "If men don't understand why we want to be separatist there's something wrong with them" was the uncompromising message (*The Abolitionist,* No. 14, 1983, p 3). Ros Kane who had founded RAP was also engaged, but critical, arguing that WIP's call for better funding for alternatives to prison was welcome, but not strong enough, and some of its other recommendations like incorporating the Prison Medical Service into the NHS, seemed more like a positive than a negative reform (*The Abolitionist,* No. 20, 1985).

On the other hand, RAP did learn from WIP, and from other women's groups, Women Against Rape in particular, which carried on a critical dialogue with RAP's sex offences working group in the early 1980s. What this revealed was that the connection between patriarchy and capitalism was not simple, and that State power was not just a mirror reflection of either.

So, no longer did the world appear to be neatly and easily divided between the powerful and the powerless in economic terms, but it was fractured along gender and ethnic lines as well. The crimes of the powerful, therefore, could not be only thought of as the economically powerful governing at the expense of the poor, along the lines of traditional class politics, but also had to be interpreted in terms of the power exercised by men over women, by white people over black people and so forth. In short, the world became a little more complicated.

However, it is arguable that women's groups played a far bigger role in penal affairs than simply re-educating RAP and it is their wider role concerning victims that I now wish to uncover as the final site of my mobile archaeology.

VICTIMS

We saw in my first essay that the plight of victims had been largely ignored in the reform agenda. Where they had been involved, it was at the margins, through the introduction of the Criminal Injuries Compensation Board which had been credited, in part at least, as a sop to convince the public that the penal reform lobby was interested in more than just the welfare of offenders. This neglect was carried through well into the 1970s and the 1980s. One of the senior civil servants at the centre of making criminal justice policy at the Home Office during this time, David Faulkner, has conceded the point (Rock 1990). As before, this neglect was partly based on the fear of officials that stressing the plight of victims might encourage the growth of vigilantism, though the cost of providing a decent service to victims was also a consideration (Rock 1990) and it continues to be.

It was therefore pressure from below that was needed to bring this particular group of outsiders into consideration, and the role of women's groups was highly significant. Briefly, the women's movement in the 1970s had defined its struggle around the issue of equal rights and it succeeded in securing anti-discrimination legislation in a number of important fields, such as employment law and wages. However, towards the end of the 1970s a number of women's groups came to the conclusion that their problem was not simply a question of discrimination, but of oppression, not least in the home and on the streets, and this led the development of a number of local groups springing up around the issues of domestic violence, rape and incest.

The first refuge for women suffering from domestic violence was set up in Chiswick in 1972 by Erin Pizzey. It became the subject of much publicity and other refuges were quickly established so that by 1985 it was reported that 150 refuges, identified by a single piece of research, had provided shelter for over 11,000 women and over 20,000 children between 1977 and 1978 (Walklate 1989, p 139). The rapid expansion of the movement reflected the obvious fact that domestic violence was hardly policed—"domestics" were not proper police work—and local social service provision for those wishing to escape violent male partners was poor or non-existent. Men were not allowed into refuges, women themselves provided mutual self-help and "counselling" in a power sharing context. Many refuges later became attached to the National Federation of Women's Aid.

If domestic violence was poorly policed in the 1970s, this was even more true of rape. Many women victims felt violated by the interrogations they were subjected to by the police, often male police. (The full force of this was later brought home to millions of viewers in Roger Graef's 1982 BBC television documentary showing a rape victim being interviewed by the Thames Valley Police.) Even if they survived this encounter, then their experience before the courts was not that much better (Soothill and Walby 1991). In order to help these victims Rape Crisis Centres sprang up. The first was opened in London in 1976; by 1983 there were six across the country. Apart from offering medical support and free legal advice, depending on what an individual victim wanted, comfort and support were offered and coping strategies worked out (Walklate 1989). There was a lot of emphasis on listening, which was likewise crucial in the development of incest support groups in the mid-1980s; here incest victims could talk through their experience outside of the family and the inhibiting "authority" that it represented.

It is important to remember two things about these groups, or movements might be a better term. The first is that their politics were dynamic and contested. For example, Erin Pizzey fell out with the feminist movement and the labelling of some women as "victims" came to be challenged and the designation "survivors" was preferred by some, instead. Second, the more militant among these groups were not prepared to engage with the Home Office, rather like RAP and WIP they feared co-option. Rock writes:

> Appeals were made directly to women and to feminists, and other groups were ignored. There was a refusal to compromise principle and practice. Theirs was the distance of the lobby that would not be "house trained". Taking to the streets, subjecting the Home Secretary to a mock trial, refusing to have much commerce with men, and barring men from entering one's buildings reinforced a moral and symbolic *cordon sanitaire* that kept the staid and respectable political world at bay. In short, certain forms of feminist activism could be read as the insignia of the disrespectful pressure group that cannot and will not enter the circle of the Home Office and government. Only one Home Office official could recall encountering a representative organization concerned with the victimization of women, and he had presented evidence to the 1975 Select Committee on violence in marriage.

(Rock 1990, p 183)

Rock's judgement about such groups is politically naïve; it says nothing about the genuine tactical complexities that faced women in engaging with the male dominated political process. However, it is certainly true that while these movements were busy with the difficult political task of hammering the plight of women victims into the public consciousness, there were other groups pushing the interest of victims in less gendered ways who were more willing to become engaged.

These groups began operating in and around the Bristol area which was where a number of influential figures in the penal lobby were based in the 1970s. Jim Little (Bristol RAP), for example, compiled the annual Ball and Chain Award for the most punitive magistrate's bench, while Philip Priestly was carrying out pioneering work with Bristol NACRO.

It was the latter, alongside Charles Irvine, who first helped to pioneer the idea of supporting victims. This began in the context of bringing offenders and victims together as a step towards some form of mediation. However, this complex agenda was soon succeeded by a more pragmatic one which was directed mainly at giving victims of crime—men and women—practical and emotional support in more routine ways, say in response to a burglary or a theft. By 1973 a National Victims' Association had been formally established, and a year later the Bristol Victims' Scheme project was set up with the support of the local police. This succeeded in getting hundreds of referrals for its volunteers to respond to (Rock 1990).

It was from these fairly modest beginnings that the National Association of Victims' Support Schemes (NAVSS) began. From the beginning the Association (eventually led by Helen Reeves) sought to reassure the Home Office that it was not much interested in offenders, about how they might be processed or sentenced, but wished to focus on giving victims practical support. It therefore posed no threat of vigilantism. Government funds eventually became available, albeit slowly, and the association, mostly on a volunteer basis, became established nationwide. But if we go beyond the association *per se* provision for victims galloped apace elsewhere. For example, the Criminal Justice Act 1982 made it clear that where a court had ordered both a fine and compensation, the paying of compensation should come first. In the Criminal Justice Act 1988 courts were obliged to explain why they were not ordering compensation where it seemed, legally and on the facts, to be appropriate. Finally, of course, there was the much heralded *Victims' Charter* in 1990.

It is wise to be critical of these initiatives. The operational effectiveness of NAVSS has been questioned. Their members might respond to victims formally, but just how much contact do they make, and how useful is the quality of the advice they offer? Furthermore, the provisions of the Criminal Justice Act 1988 suggest that the idea of using compensation took more time to get going, as did some of the promised service provisions set out in the market orientated *Victims' Charter*. As far as the provision for rape victims is concerned, there is still criticism of what is available in some parts of the country, and even if more victims are prepared to come forward the number of successful criminal prosecutions for rape is unacceptably low.

So there is a long way to go. But even if we allow for such necessary qualifications, there can also be little doubt that the interests of victims of crime became inscribed on the criminal justice system in the 1970s and 1980s in a way that bears no comparison with the immediate postwar decades when victims of crime were the outsiders *par excellence*, and whose needs, when they were graciously addressed, had been determined and handed down by the great and the good serving on government committees. Victims had forced themselves onto the political agenda from below and, as best they could, they sought to announce their own agenda.

CONCLUSION

In 1987 Vivien Stern, then Director of NACRO, wrote a widely read book about the recent politics of penal change in Britain, *Bricks of Shame*. It contained no mention of the contributions made by groups like PROP, RAP or WIP to this political struggle, an omission which drew a sharp *riposte* from the guardian of PROP's legacy and its former organizer, Geoff Coggan. He deeply resented the idea that prominent outsider groups from the 1960s and 1970s were "being snuffed out of the records as if they did not exist" (*The Abolitionist*, No. 23, 1987). It is not my purpose to second guess why Vivien Stern, now Baroness Stern, made such an obvious omission, nor indeed to explore why one of the most successful academic textbooks on penal policy in Britain did much the same thing in its first edition a few years later (Cavadino and Dignan 1992).

It will be obvious, however, from what has already been argued that I think these outsider groups had—and in a sense continue to have—some influence on the politics of penal change in Britain, and therefore such omissions were not only ungenerous, particularly at the time, but more to the point, unwarranted. So my mobile archaeology has been partly intended to put this right. I intend that students and the interested public should get a different picture, one which offers them an opportunity to assess the part these groups have played. I do not want commentaries on penal change in Britain during this period to become (wrongly) a history of critical silence.

Yet, I have to concede that ignoring outsider groups when re-working the past, in much the same way as the Home Office ignored them in the 1970s and 1980s, is tempting. After all, to make the case that PROP influenced the legal struggle to secure prisoners' rights following the HMP Hull riot, that with RAP it successfully exposed control units, or that WIP helped to clean up HMP Holloway's C1 wing is to focus on some very particular successes. These were important, true, but there surely remain more searching questions to be asked and answered before we can judge the impact these outsider groups had on how penal policy was made and about the general direction of that policy. It is to these wider ranging and very difficult judgements, that I now turn, starting with the policy process.

One of the more banal and easily verifiable judgments to make, I think, is that there is little doubt that the arrival of these outsider groups, as I have defined them, signalled a significant shift in the character of the penal lobby in Britain, indicating its conversion from a policy community into an issue orientated community. What policy scientists mean by this distinction is simply this. A policy community is a lobby which is agreed on a shared set of values, where the contributing pressure groups are stable, and where contacts between government and non-government group officials are regular and easy, and where no group feels excluded. An issue orientated lobby on the other hand is unstable; some groups in it operate on a quite different set of assumptions than those in government and other lobby groups, and access is uneven. Outsider groups find life difficult; they never quite dare to penetrate the inner core of government, and engagement, even at a distance, poses difficult choices. In such lobbies the arguments are robust, public and sometimes divisive, and given the particular nature of the counter culture and later the feminist movements from which they sprang, the groups we have written about often defined *themselves* at the margins.

Clearly, on the evidence provided, groups like PROP, RAP and WIP transformed the mostly male, elite policy community which the Howard League (and later NACRO) had shared with successive Home Secretaries over many decades and which I described in *Part I*. Ideological differences were sharp throughout this period. Furthermore, the new groups brought their own knowledges from below to challenge those of the experts who had previously claimed to speak for them in the corridors of power. Issues which the groups defined as important were not always those that pre-occupied the Home Office.

Nor was there, even when there was a shared concern, an understanding about what exactly the problem was, and what might be the solution. The liberal, male, white metropolitan elite was jostled, sometimes even belittled, by more raucous and more authentic voices as the process of penal policy making became more open, more contested and more overtly political. The fact that the Home Office failed—in some cases, even refused to engage with these more radical groups—is hugely significant, of course, and I shall return to this point later, but it does not obscure the simple fact that the penal lobby enlarged and divided.

Significantly, underpinning and sustaining this transformation of the lobby were the several "alternative realities" that the new groups sought to inscribe on the criminal justice system. True, we have seen that these groups sometimes constructed different and conflicting narratives; at times they were allied to little more than righteous indignation. But righteous indignation, like that of the grieving families who have lost loved ones half-strangled in police vans or beaten up in prison cells, like Jimmy Kelly or Barry Prosser, can go a long way when combined with even half-formed theory (Coggan and Walker 1982; Scraton 1987). Who does not recall the righteous indignation of East Ender Peter Chappell—he passionately believed in the integrity of British justice—who more or less single handedly secured the release of George Davis after his wrongful arrest and imprisonment (Ryan 1983)? Who does not remember the outrage feminist groups felt when judges and the press suggested that women rape victims contributed to their fate if they had been hitch hiking (Soothill and Walby 1991)? It was the power of this alliance between reason and emotion which helped these radical groups to mount a sustained and plausible attack on the credibility (and meaning) of the criminal justice system, including the penal system.

To be sure, governments in the 1980s continued with the pretence that prison officers did not "put the boot in" fairly regularly, and refused to acknowledge that police sometimes "stitched up" their suspects, or that some police were racist, but research demonstrated that fewer and fewer members of the public believed them. In truth, PACE, the Police and Criminal Evidence Act 1984, was partly an attempt to rein in the abuse of police power when interviewing suspects as doubts surfaced over the reliability of the convictions of the Guildford Four (1974) and the Birmingham Six (1978) and the repeal of the "sus" law became inevitable.

Even the idea that the criminal justice system was politically neutral took a battering when magistrates barred pickets travelling from Kent to the Nottingham coalfields in 1984, and when police fought pitched and bloody battles with striking miners (Fine and Millar 1985). Whatever the disputed reality might have been, Roger Graef makes my point when he observes:

> The shot of a bobby hitting a miner over the head with his truncheon became a national image. Phalanxes of police in riot gear were seen attacking apparently unprotected miners who seemed to be trying to escape. Even for the viewers with pro-police sympathies, it was a disturbing sight.
>
> (Graef 1989, p 72)

This exercise of naked force, and the inequalities of power it suggested, were reinforced when police pay packets, swelled by overtime payments, were deliberately waved in the faces of the striking miners. Within months PROP was invited to address the National Association of Miners in Prison at a meeting in Barnsley where Geoff Coggan teased out the relationship between the imprisoned miners and other groups in society: Irish political activists and young blacks who had been swept into Young Offender Institutions following the Brixton and Toxteth uprisings. 'No one would have ever have guessed I would be here', he mused (*The Abolitionist*, No. 19, 1985).

The significance of these developments should not be underestimated. What I mean by this is that the hegemony that the ruling groups, powerful men, mostly white men, had secured in this area, their capacity to convince the public that

British justice was politically neutral, even handed and humane, "the best in the world", had been almost unassailable in the postwar period. Indeed, this was seen to be one of the admired peculiarities of the British since the eighteenth century (Thompson 1978; Hay 1977). I do not, obviously, wish to suggest that between the late 1960s and into the first part of the 1980s the alternative narratives I have excavated in *Part II* were widely held, or that they replaced the dominant view—the bourgeois view as some RAP members would have put it—about the nature of our criminal justice system. On the contrary, the groups that I have written about often had only a few hundred members, and were in many ways unrepresentative of the public as a whole. Nonetheless, through their arguments and their practice, backed up and supported by a less deferential political culture, they helped to disturb the complacency that had surrounded the operation of the criminal justice system in Britain and to undermine the self-confidence of those who ran it.

The exact nature of the changes they secured, however, is not easy to characterize, even with the value of hindsight. To put the question more directly, if the criminal justice system was not transformed by these critiques just how was it changed? The best answer I can give is that *these alternative critiques penetrated the system rather than transformed it, helping to disturb and change it, though without disrupting its essential rationale or deep purpose.* Let me illustrate the nature of this change with the example of prisons.

During the second half of the 1980s the Home Office began a long series of consultations about the future shape of the criminal justice system which culminated in the publication of its landmark White Paper, *Crime, Justice and Protecting the Public* (HMSO 1990). In the course of that White Paper it was suggested that "nobody now regards imprisonment, in itself, as an effective means of reform for most offenders". Indeed, it went on to assert, famously, that imprisonment was "an expensive means of making bad people worse" (para 2.7).

While RAP would never have suggested that all prisoners are necessarily "bad people", this was just the message about imprisonment it had been trying to get across to both Labour and Conservative governments—and the Howard League—since 1970, demanding that alternatives to custody be developed instead of prisons whose numbers could be significantly reduced, possibly even abolished altogether. It is true, of course, that the government's own Advisory Council on the Penal System had come out in favour of providing more alternatives at about the same time RAP came into being (Home Office 1970).

So RAP's voice was not the only one that was being heard, nor was it necessarily the most influential one. For example, as alternatives were thought to offer serious cost savings over imprisonment, there is probably something in the argument that the Home Office was responding to the Treasury. So material factors played a part, but RAP's almost evangelical certainty about the failure of prison reform was an ever present voice in the penal lobby forcing the Howard League and NACRO to question their certainties about the prison system. Also, the debate about the principles on which any new alternatives to custody might be based was infused by RAP's critical challenge, which a number of young idealistic probation officers took up.

The fact that RAP and its supporters did not win this particular debate, or secure its wider vision of a less punitive world without prison, is pretty obvious. The prison system marched onwards, expanding, and alternatives to custody grew at the same time, so widening the net, and also becoming progressively more punitive (Cohen 1985). However, what is important for our present argument is to acknowledge that RAP was a *distinctive voice contributing to this process of penal change*. By focusing on the penal system's many hidden purposes, its function in relation to wider social processes, and alongside PROP and WIP, exposing the system's enduring capacity to inflict brutalities, RAP made a positive contribution *even as its radical message was being subsumed and transformed into a more conservative one*. To "snuff out" its contribution, as Geoff Coggan phrased it, was simply to misunderstand how social processes work.

RAP and other groups like Justice for Children, alongside radical prisoners' movements in Scandinavia and America, also contributed to the rise of the so-called justice model (Hudson 1987). What this suggested was that if prisons did not reform, if the "treatment model" now lacked credibility, then offenders should be sentenced according to the seriousness of their offence, on the basis of their "just desserts", not on the spurious argument that they might be released early by the executive when they were judged by their therapists to have "peaked" in their training (Bottoms 1980). That these groups supported this emphasis on "punishment," pure and simple, rather than on "permissive" rehabilitation, coincided and reinforced the New Right's emerging agenda around repression, incapacitation and mangerialism, reveals the *paradoxes or ironies* inherent in most processes of social change. These need to be articulated rather than ignored; no penal narrative is plausible without them.

If this sounds too pessimistic, I would repeat that even where radical groups found their basic principles subverted and transformed to serve what they felt were establishment purposes, some gains were secured. So, for example, Walklate and Mawby (1994) agree that the "androgynous" NAVSS has enabled the State to co-opt some of the issues raised by the women's movement, so that women's needs "are being met in such a way as they no longer constitute a challenge to the State," but nonetheless many of the provisions still represent gains for women victims. The same outcome can likewise be claimed for other struggles around the penal system, especially the prison, as I have been at pains to point out.

Finally, it is important to remember that the politics of the counter culture which I took as the starting point and strategic inspiration for my examination of outsider groups had subsided by the mid-1970s. Nonetheless, as we have seen its legacy of working from below, of emphasizing the personal over the political, of mobilizing campaigns outside of formal State structures, to some extent endured, not least among many feminist groups and at least some, if not all, of the more militant groups founded by the GLC until its demise in 1984. The politics that overlaid it, however, though never entirely replacing it, in the second half of the 1970s was of an altogether different kind, and partly explains how PROP travelled the distance from HMP Brixton to Barnsley in just a few years.

After the demise of the social contract which had attempted to counter the inflationary impact of the oil crisis in 1974, the consequent return of mass unemployment, the rise of the National Front and the violent impact of Irish nationalism on the mainland, Britain seemed like an island under siege. While it is true that the quadrupling of oil prices and the impact of international terrorism were also felt elsewhere in Europe, the crisis was arguably experienced more deeply in Britain and saw the emergence of the New Right with its agenda built around the need for stronger social discipline.

The impact of the New Right has been mostly analysed in terms of its populist appeal, its mobilization of a peculiar British form of authoritarian populism around the "strong state" (Hall *et al.* 1978; Scraton P. (ed.) 1987). In this climate, the politics of the counter culture, even the modest legislative liberalism of the 1960s which had secured homosexual and abortion law reform, came to be inscribed with the iconography of moral laxness, if not decay. How this populist sentiment was generated is an important line of intellectual inquiry about the politics of the 1970s and the early 1980s, including its impact on penal policy, and I shall return to populism in my final essay. It has a continuing echo.

However, in the next essay I want to begin by looking at the impact that the New Right had on the structure and operation of the penal system from the late 1980s onwards in the context of privatization and managerialism. These debates, and the innovations they generated, seem very different from the grand ideological struggles we have been examining here, but they are not quite as narrow as they seem, and what is more, they had a significant impact on the way the penal system was structured and the way its services, as we are now invited to call them, were delivered.

REFERENCES for *Part II*

Bottoms A.E. and Preston R. H. (1980) *The Coming Penal Crisis* (Edinburgh: Scottish Academic Press)
Box-Grainger J. (1983) "A New Strategy?" *The Abolitionist*, No. 12, pp 14-21
Carlen P. (1985) *Criminal Women* (London: Polity)
Cavadino M. and Dignan J. (1992) *The Penal System* (London: Sage)
Christie N. (1982) *The Limits of Pain* (London: Martin Robertson)
Coggan G. and Walker M. (1982) *Frightened For My Life* (London: Fontana)
Cohen S. (1972) *Folk Devils and Moral Panics* (London: MacGibbon and Kee)
Cohen S (1974) "Criminology and the Sociology of Deviance in Britain" in Rock P. and McIntosh M. (eds.) *Deviance and Social Control* (London: Tavistock)
Cohen S. and Taylor L. (1978) *Prison Secrets* (London: NCCL and RAP)
Cohen S. (1979) *Crime and Punishment* (London: RAP)
Cohen S. (1985) *Visions of Social Control* (London: Polity Press)
Crick B. *The Reform of Parliament* (London: Weidenfeld and Nicolson)
Dronfield L. (1908) *Outside Chance: The Story of the Newham Alternatives Project* (London: RAP)
Faulkner D. (2001) *Crime, State and Citizen: A Field Full of Folk* (Winchester: Waterside Press)
Fine B. and Millar R. (1985) *Policing the Miners' Strike* (London: Lawrence and Wishart)
Fitzgerald M. (1977) *Prisoners in Revolt* (Harmondsworth: Penguin)
Fitzgerald M. and Sim J. (1979) *British Prisons* (Oxford: Blackwell)
Foucault M. (1980) *Power/Knowledge* (Brighton: Harvester)
Graef R. (1989) *Talking Blues* (London: Fontana)
Hall S. *et al* (1978) *Policing the Crisis* (London: Macmillan)
Hay D. *et al* (1976) *Albion's Fatal Tree* (Harmondsworth: Penguin)
HMSO (1968) *The Civil Service* (Cmnd 3638)
HMSO (1990) *Crime, Justice and Protecting the Public* (Cmnd 965)
Home Office (1970) *Non Custodial and Semi-Custodial Sentences* (London: Home Office)
Hudson B. (1987) *Justice Through Welfare* (London: Macmillan)
Irwin J. (1989) *Western Europe since 1945* (London: Longman)
King J. F. S. and Jarvis F. (1977) "The Influence of the Probation and Aftercare Service" in Walker N. (ed.) *Penal Policy Making in England* (Cambridge: Institute of Criminology)
Livingstone S. and Owen T. (1993) *Prison Law* (Oxford: Clarendon)
Mathiesen T. (1974) *The Politics of Abolition* (London: Martin Robertson)
Mawby R. I. and Walklate S. (1994) *Critical Victimology* (London: Sage)
Musgrove T. (1974) *Ecstasy and Holiness* (London: Methuen)
Nelson E. (1989) *The British Counter Culture 1966-73: A Study of the Underground Press* (London: Macmillan)
Pearson G. (1983) *Hooligan: a History of Respectable Fears* (London: Macmillan)
PROP (1977) *Don't Mark His Face* (London: PROP)

Radzinowicz L. (1999) *Adventures in Criminology* (London: Routledge)

RAP (1972) *Alternatives to Holloway* (London: Radical Alternatives to Prison)

Rock P. (1990) *Helping Victims of Crime* (Oxford: Clarendon Press)

Rock P. (1998) *After Homicide* (Oxford: Clarendon Press)

Ryan M. (1996) *Lobbying From Below: INQUEST in Defence of Civil Liberties* (London: UCL Press)

Ryan M. and Ward T. (1992) "From Positivism to Postmodernism: Some Theoretical and Strategic Reflections on the Evolution of the Penal Lobby in Britain" *International Journal of the Sociology of Law*, Vol. 20, 321–335

Ryan M. (1978) *The Acceptable Pressure Group: A Case Study of the Howard League and Radical Alternatives to Prison* (Farnborough: Teakfield)

Scott D. and Whitfield D. (1993) *Paying Back: Twenty Years of Community Service* (Winchester: Waterside Press)

Scraton P. (ed.) (1987) *Law, Order and the Authoritarian State* (Milton Keynes: Open University Press)

Soothill K. and Walby S. (1991) *Sex Crime in the News* (London: Routledge)

Supple B. (1994) "British Economic Decline since 1945" in *The Economic History of Britain since 1870* Floud R. and McClosky D. (eds.) second edition (Cambridge: Cambridge University Press)

Taylor I., Walton P. and Young J. (1974) *The New Criminology* (London: Routledge and Kegan Paul)

Taylor R. and Young N. (1987) (eds.) *Campaigns for Peace* (Manchester: Manchester University Press)

Thompson E. P. (1975) *Whigs and Hunters* (London: Allen Lane)

Walkate S. (1989) *Victimology* (London: Unwin Hyman)

Ward T. (1991) "Rediscovering Radical Alternatives" in Lasocik Z., Platek M. and Rzeplinska I. (eds.) *Abolitionism in History* (Warsaw: Warsaw University)

PART III

Managers and Managerialism

In this third essay I want to trace how the structure and management of the penal system were substantially changed, some may wish even to argue they were transformed, in the 1990s.

For example, the monopoly held by the public sector over the delivery of punishment at the hard end of the system was effectively ended with the opening in 1992 of Britain's first privately managed prison for more than a century. In the same year the management of the Prison Service was distanced from political control with the creation of the Prison Service Agency. Under the guidance of its new Chief Executive, recruited from the private sector and well versed in new private sector management techniques, the Agency was to be allowed to get on with the day-to-day business of managing prisons, that is, free from interfering politicians and senior civil servants at the Home Office.

These radical changes were at first contested at an ideological level by many politicians, civil servants, and most penal lobby groups, and more pragmatically by some stakeholders in the system, like prison officers who feared job losses. Nor were the changes always easily secured, or maintained without embarrassment, and adjustments were necessary. Furthermore, while this might appear at first sight to be a de-centralising agenda, the management techniques introduced to monitor better the performance of new corporate and individual operatives in the penal field arguably strengthened the authority of the "new" system at the centre rather than weakened it.

The Probation Service saw a somewhat different process at work, with power shifting more transparently to the centre. Local probation services were forced to comply with a National Statement of Objectives, leaving little manoeuvre for local priorities; their training was radically overhauled away from social work practice, and finally, the structure of their local management areas came to be more directly controlled by the Home Secretary.

The context in which many of these changes took place was the political agenda which came to be associated with the growing ascendancy of the New Right from the mid-1970s onwards. This sought to reduce the size of central government, to hollow it out, and hive off a whole range of government services either through privatization under new competitive, regulatory frameworks, or by the creation of new government agencies once removed from government under the rubric of Next Steps. By the late 1970s big, top down, bureaucratic government was no longer good government. In particular, the hierarchical Welfare State, managed by Civil Service mandarins who had spent their lives in the public service, and whose considerable power and influence I outlined in Part I, was being seriously contested. While the services that it offered were in some senses unique, provoking some very particular arguments, the remodelling of the penal system was part of this wider process of disaggregation and managerial reform.

Why some politicians thought this remodelling to be necessary is something that I shall deal with early on to give some contextual meaning to prison privatization and the new managerialism.

CONTINUITY WITH ADJUSTMENT

In *Part II* I argued that the "alternative realities" presented by a whole range of outsider groups from the late 1960s into the mid-1980s did have some impact on the way the criminal justice system was viewed. An archaeology of their achievement in helping to undermine the self-confidence of those who ran the system was therefore more than justified.

I did not suggest, however, that the traditional objectives and deep structures of the penal system were seriously threatened at that time, though they may have been *adjusted*. So, while the idea of reparation began to be taken seriously, and there was an early intellectual flirtation with the idea of "justice", when policy makers spoke publicly about the purposes of the penal system they still mostly talked in terms of deterrence, retribution, punishment and, though with increasing uncertainty it is true, about rehabilitation or reform. The May Report (HMSO 1979, Cmnd 7673) into the Prison Service, for example, wrestled very uncomfortably with the suggestion that *all* the service might offer was "humane containment". (It is worth noting here that this report did not give prisoners a voice.) At a structural level, alternatives to prison began to proliferate, it is true, including the distant possibility of electronic tagging, yet in 1983 the government also announced the biggest prison building programme since Victorian times (Ryan and Sim 1998). Both the contours and the purposes of the old penal system therefore stayed in place.

Senior civil servants remained confident, in spite of the many problems they had encountered in the 1970s, that they would continue to manage the penal system, especially prisons, much as they always had done. This was clear in their evidence to the May inquiry. Home Office officials were at pains to stress the Prison Service's singular achievements over almost a century, the complexities of its many tasks, and above all else, their confidence that it would continue to operate as a public service. They argued:

> The government is answerable to Parliament, and through Parliament to the electorate. The present arrangements provide direct ministerial control over these services that have the responsibility for the treatment of those members of the community who are placed compulsorily in custody. *Public and Parliamentary interest seems certain to require that the Prison Service should remain as a public service to ensure that the present system of accountability would remain in some form and undiminished rigour.*
>
> (HMSO 1979C, Vol. 1, p 4) (Emphasis added)

We know in retrospect that this was complacent, and that within a decade there were plans to unscramble the Home Office and to introduce private prisons. However, my purpose in mentioning this here is not to claim the advantage of hindsight, but simply to point out that the Home Office was resolutely committed to the idea of a highly centralized public service. Its officials, one might say, were steeped in that tradition, and to move outside of it was to "think the unthinkable".

The policy making process showed the same pattern of *continuity*, though again with some *adjustment*. For example, the cosy interchange between senior civil servants, expert academics and practitioners, was to a degree upset by the surprise decision of the Thatcher government in 1979 not to reappoint the Advisory Council on the Penal System (ACPS). A more accountable window on penal policy-making became available with the introduction of Parliamentary Select Committees, and the Home Affairs Select Committee through its public hearings quickly became influential.

However, a modified patterning of informal, behind the scenes networking was quickly established in place of ACPS between senior civil servants, representatives from the "established" penal lobby groups like NACRO and the Howard League and academic experts who would meet regularly to review policy developments. Business was conducted informally: talk and argument over wine and sandwiches. Roy King, one of the senior academics involved in these regular meetings at NACRO premises or in Whitehall itself gives us their flavour. The discussions he says:

> ... were confidential in the sense that no one would have wished to embarrass another member of the group by repeating things better not said in public, but if the discussion stimulated ideas for an article or for an initiative within the Prison Department, so much the better ... Virtually no subject was excluded from the agenda of the meetings, and as the members of the group developed understanding and mutual respect so there was an unprecedented sharing of data and ideas, with opinions vigorously and freely expressed.
>
> (King and McDermott 1995, pp 3-4)

The group contained some very senior and influential academics, including the later to be knighted Anthony Bottoms who was by then Director of the Cambridge Institute of Criminology. However, the number of non-Oxbridge academics in this elite *ensemble* had increased, reflecting the expansion of criminology teaching and research in British universities since the 1950s. These meetings were the initiative of civil servant David Faulkner who rose to become Deputy Permanent Under Secretary at the Home Office (Rutherford 1996; King and McDermott 1995; Windlesham 1993). Faulkner had been educated at Oxford where he read classics.

The traditional authority of senior civil servants was not much diluted by this new arrangement. This may seem strange given the powerful critique that was mounted against the higher Civil Service by the Royal Commission (Fulton) in 1966 which accused it of being elitist, closed and amateurish. This critique, however, was so successfully neutered by the Whitehall machine that ten years later the service still showed a significant Oxbridge bias with a preference for the generalist administrator educated in classics or history whose all round intellectual abilities had been supposedly identified in the controversial studies by Sir Cyril Burt into "general intelligence" (Kellner and Crowther Hunt 1980). The power of the Civil Service was, therefore, still entrenched in the 1970s, so much so that at the start of the 1980s Mrs Thatcher's problems in securing change were said to have exact "parallels to those faced by the Fulton reformers [a generation earlier], how to engage the commitment of a government machine that is both the agent and the object of reform" (Kellner and Crowther Hunt 1980).

It was in Faulkner's *ensemble* that the justice model first received a sustained hearing in policy making circles, and where the seeds of the Criminal Justice Act

1991 were sown. This was intended as an extremely progressive piece of legislation, particularly section 29 of the Act which provided that offenders should be sentenced on the basis of the offence for which they were before the courts and not on the basis of their previous convictions. It was expected that this would reduce the length of many sentences. Also included in its provisions was the unit fine scheme which attempted to link fines to an offender's means to pay. In short, middle-class offenders should at last begin to pay fines according to their sometimes considerable means.

It has to be admitted that this legislation proved to be deeply unpopular among some magistrates, magistrates' clerks and some Conservative backbenchers (Dunbar and Langdon 1998).[1] As a result, under the Criminal Justice Act 1993, the unit fine scheme was quickly dropped, as were two key sentencing rules which had been introduced by the 1991 Act: the bar on previous convictions or responses to earlier sentences being taken into account when assessing the seriousness of the present offence; and the limitation under which only one other associated offence could be taken into account. However, the 1991 Act remains a powerful symbol of the power of the reconstituted, liberal metropolitan elite at the centre of the policy making process in England to impress its ideas on government. The fact that many people, including in fairness it has to be said, one or two members of Faulkner's liberal *ensemble*, were not entirely convinced by it, did not prevent it from reaching the statute book under one of the most conservative administrations in recent times. (I will elaborate on the unstable environment in which this Act was processed later.)

The process of change I have just outlined illustrates that there were some *adjustments* made to penal structures, and to penal policy making processes, in Britain during the first decade of the Conservative ascendancy, but that these coexisted with many *continuities*. This was to change in the late 1980s when there was more of a *fracture*, though never a complete break. To understand these changes, and to assess their impact on the way the penal system was both structured and managed, we need to look at the rise of the New Right in the 1970s, to trace its influence on the overall political context and operation of government.

THE POLITICS OF THE NEW RIGHT

In *Part I* I pointed out that although Britain may not have done as well as its European neighbours in the 1950s and 1960s it had nevertheless achieved sustained economic growth. This was to come to an abrupt end with the oil crisis in 1973, and from then until 1988 there was a significant and marked decline in Britain's economic performance. Real output per worker and productivity grew far more slowly, and there were corresponding rises in the rates of inflation and unemployment (Feinstein 1994). These circumstances led to serious social unrest, to which I have previously alluded and to which I shall return in my final essay on *Populism*. In the meantime, however, I want to explore how the New Right interpreted this decline and how they sought to put it right, starting with the idea of *Overload*.

---

[1]   The Magistrates' Association and Justices' Clerks' Society remained committed to unit fines; making this clear to the Home Secretary and his advisors at the time.

The New Right's starting point was that government had become over complex because it was too big. In 1977 Richard Rose observed that:

One cause of organizational over-complexity can be diagnosed as the growth of government. Whatever indicator is used, in every western nation the proportion of government employees has increased substantially since the War, and so too has the size of public expenditure, both in absolute terms and as a share of the country's Gross National Product. The number of government departments has been growing too ... Governments are trying to do more things ...

(Rose 1977)

One consequence of governments trying to do more than they can manage, it was claimed, is that they do things inefficiently.

However, and this was the crucial next step for the New Right, in order to sustain this *Overload* governments had been forced to raise public expenditure, particularly to support non-productive welfare provision. This drain on productive industry, on the wealth creating sectors of the economy, and on the over taxed consumer, had only been possible when western economies were growing and the State could live off its "fiscal dividend". Now this solvent had dried up and the "fiscal crisis" was upon us (O'Connor 1973). Governments needed to offer fewer services, and ensure that those that remained were efficiently delivered, or face the alternative of imposing penal rates of tax on private capital—and consumers—which would still further reduce economic growth. Printing money as a way out of meeting this deficit was, argued Milton Friedman, simply a recipe for inflation (MacInnes 1987). In shorthand, Keynesian analysis was being edged out by Monetarism.

In identifying this as the 1970s politics of the New Right I do not seek to hide the fact that there was a certain symmetry between the analysis I have presented here and more traditional Marxist interpretations of the crisis. For example, influential European figures on the Left like Habermas (1976) also recognized that the historic postwar compromise between capital and labour which I referred to in *Part I* that had secured (and financed) the Welfare State was floundering; that the State's inherently contradictory role, as Marxists saw it, of having to serve the interests of capital accumulation, yet at the same time secure social harmony, was at a point of crisis.

In Britain the rhetoric—as opposed to an analysis—of the crisis was cogently expressed by Conservative Party ideologist Sir Keith Joseph in 1979 in a pamphlet written for the Centre for Policy Studies:

The visible signs of Britain's unique course—as it slides from the affluent western world towards the threadbare economies of the communist bloc—are obvious enough. We have a demotivating tax system, increasing nationalization, compressed differentials, low and stagnant productivity, high unemployment, many failing public services and inexorably growing central government expenditure; an obsession with equality and with pay, price and dividend controls; a unique set of privileges and immunities for trade unions; and finally, since 1974, top of the western league of inflation, bottom of the league for growth.

(Quoted in Gamble 1990, p 127)

Added to these signs of crisis the New Right later pointed to the "dependency culture" that the "nanny State" had allegedly induced among its citizens who now expected generous Welfare State "handouts" from the cradle to the grave. This not only contributed towards "Big Government" by enlarging welfare bureaucracies, it was doing something even worse, undermining individual self-reliance.

Of course, it is one thing to identify a crisis and another thing to tackle it. The truth of the matter is that party ideologists—of the Left or Right—rarely present well formed or programmatic offerings. Their contributions are better understood as the beginning of a process rather than a finished product. I make this point because the analysis I have sketched out here would have suggested—at the very least—a large scale and immediate programme of de-nationalization, or privatization as we would now call it, once Mrs Thatcher was voted into power in 1979. In fact, this did *not* happen. Indeed, there was no mention of any such programme in the Conservative Party election manifesto in 1979. Furthermore, given that Left and Right were agreed there was a "fiscal crisis" it might reasonably be expected that Mrs Thatcher's first administration would have substantially reduced public expenditure. In fact, her government actually *increased* it.

This demonstrates several things. The first is that re-modelling the postwar Welfare State, and the political consensus that underpinned it, at first involved considerable government outlay because of the unemployment it generated. Second, policing the social dislocation that re-structuring caused was also expensive and it was therefore necessary to commit even more resources to law and order. Third, though less striking than the apparent paradox I have just explained, is the banal truth that re-structuring the great ship of State takes time.

Setting the people free

It was, therefore, not until after the 1983 General Election that the Conservative government began "setting the people free," as the Americans put it, by first selling off a whole range of publicly owned utilities, such as telecommunications, gas, electricity and, later, water. As monopolies these utilities were argued to be inherently inefficient, and made more so by being directed by Whitehall civil servants who knew little or nothing about business. They should therefore be hived off and subject to the competition of the market place. This would reduce "Big Government" at a stroke. And to an extent it did, with the symbolic closing down of the Parliamentary Select Committee whose task had been to oversee Whitehall's administration of the nationalized industries; its role was defunct.

However, these privatizations initially meant that large players, sometimes monopoly players, were released into the market place, and so while the government had indeed divested itself of direct control over their operations, it needed to regulate their practices by instituting a whole raft of regulators to oversee the operation of these industries, fixing prices, monitoring long term investment plans and so forth. This surveillance caused problems and sometimes led to public quarrels.

In some cases it was claimed that the regulators had been colonized by their industry. Nobody now believes that Railtrack was properly regulated in the 1990s, for example, and more than one regulator was eased out of office. So government did not disappear, or relinquish control, it simply changed its role, operating at a distance to secure a competitive market place.

This model of restructuring the post-war State is the one that most people in Britain are familiar with. Many people will have bought shares in these former nationalized industries, British Gas, British Steel, for example, when they were launched onto the market in the mid-1980s. However, this model for change should be understood as an early one that applied mostly to industry and commerce. Changes to remodel the Welfare State came later. In fact, it is arguable that the development of the New Public Management (NPM) techniques—mostly borrowed from America—which were to have such a profound effect on the way the penal system and other social services were structured and managed only really began to make themselves felt at the Home Office at about the same time as civil servants began the detailed planning of what was to become the Criminal Justice Act 1991.

It is to New Public Management (NPM) and how it brought about a *fracture*, though not a complete break, in the way the penal system was structured and managed that I now turn, though again this too has to be introduced and understood in a wider context.

New public management: the basics
We have already learnt that Conservatives were far from happy with the Welfare State. As they saw things, it was over staffed, more bureaucratic than it needed to be, and its services were altogether too expensive for the taxpayer. It was at these services, those that could not easily be off loaded onto the market place, that the NPM programme was directed in the 1980s (Rhodes 1997). The programme had two elements.

The first, new institutional economics, stressed the need to disaggregate the big Whitehall Welfare bureaucracies and to create greater choice by contracting out the services they offered to the private sector and instituting quasi-markets to stimulate consumer choice and reduce costs. One way of achieving this would be to offer these bureaucracies agency status, distancing them from direct government control. There was sometimes opposition to this in particular instances, to the creation of an internal market among hospital trusts in the NHS, for example.

The second element of NPM was introducing private sector management practices into the public sector. This required explicit standards to be set, targets identified and performance measured. Taken together these two elements were intended to transform the delivery and efficiency of welfare services and help to reduce the fiscal deficit.

I hope it is now clear that re-modelling the State following the breakdown of the postwar consensus was a gradual process involving more than one model; that attempting to replace the State by the market as the provider of many of its services was a complicated process, as well a highly contested one, and that it touched just about very aspect of our public life. It was this wider context, the debate about the nature and role of government (or governance), that gave meaning to, was the motor for, the contested *fracture* that took place in the penal system in the late 1980s and 1990s.

Those who ran Britain's penal system were to be as much disturbed by these New Right "alternative realities" as they had been disturbed by the "alternative realities" of the Counter Culture, arguably more so.

PRISON PRIVATIZATION: RHETORIC AND REALITY

New Right rhetoric

Helping the New Right in the late 1970s to articulate its ideological message, and seriously to think through some of the policy implications of that message, were a number of think tanks, the most high profile of which was the Centre for Policy Studies mentioned earlier in connection with Sir Keith Joseph. Another, but altogether less well known think tank at the time, was the Adam Smith Institute (ASI) which had originally been financed by the American New Right. It was from this source, as part of a larger *Omega Project* into free market economics, that the idea of private prisons first appeared in Britain in 1984, at about the same time as the Conservative government's privatization of the great public utilities was getting under way. *Justice Policy* (ASI 1984) was in some respects a thoughtful, reflective report, but it had little to say about private prisons *per se* other than to *assert* that the private sector might bring innovative management techniques and through capital investment improve technology to help to reduce the cost of prison places. The Institute's report therefore had little impact, except among the curious like myself. However, in 1987 the Institute published another report, *The Prison Cell* (ASI 1987), authored by Peter Young, which explained the *already* established virtues of American private prisons which Britain was urged to adopt.

By this time the idea of private prisons was beginning to move up the political agenda, but it has to be said that it was still not taken very seriously, not even by those close to the Prime Minister. So when the possibility was first raised in Parliament, the then Conservative Home Secretary, Douglas Hurd, was confident that few people would

> accept a case for auctioning or privatizing the prisons or handing over the business of keeping prisoners safe from anyone other than government servants.

> (*Hansard*, col. 1303, 16 July 1987)

This caution was justified, not least because at this time, and indeed, well after the clauses that eventually allowed for private prisons had been enshrined in the Criminal Justice Act 1991, the argument was more rhetorical than factual.

Take, for example, Peter Young's claim in *The Prison Cell* to have conducted a "comprehensive review" of prison privatization in America. In truth, this seems to have been based on no more than a few telephone calls, newspaper reports, conversations with the Corrections Corporation of America (CCA) and the representatives of two firms that had expressed their willingness to finance private sector prisons. The only detailed, critical research into a private sector institution at that time, carried out by the National Institute of Corrections into Okeechobee, a non-profit making institution for young boys, receives very scant attention. Young is more interested in telling us about a favourable newspaper report on a jail in Sante Fe, a report incidentally which was published before the jail was formally handed over to the private sector in the form of the CCA. As for Young's methods of analysing cost savings, these were of a type judged to be "almost useless" by a fervent advocate of prison privatization who had served on President Reagan's Commission on Privatization, and who was later to publish with the ASI (Ryan and Ward 1989, p 46).

There is also, throughout Young's cleverly ambiguous report, a sense of dynamism; the feeling that America is on course for an imminent and massive expansion in prison privatization; that this will soon penetrate the core of the prison system, go beyond managing a few local jails, or facilities for low risk immigrant detainees and juveniles. Yet, even by 1993, some six years after Young's report was published, the most generous estimate of the number of prisoners held in private sector prisons, jails and detention centres in America was around 30,000 out of a total prison population of over one and a quarter million (Ryan 1993).

This capacity to talk up the experience of other countries was also demonstrated by Members of Parliament. For example, in a Standing Committee debate on the privatization clauses of what became the Criminal Justice Act 1991, a Conservative supporter of the New Right argued that:

> The Right Honourable gentleman's point about the way forward for the Prison Service, if he believes that lower wages for the employees would be detrimental to the service provided to prisoners, he should consider events in the United States and Australia. Private sector prisons there have lower rates of recidivism than those in the public sector.
>
> (*Hansard*, Standing Committee A, col. 575, 31 January 1991)

There was no evidence for such a claim. Indeed, the Australian private prison at Borallon had only just opened.

Similar misinformation, though not quite as blatant it is true, can be found in a report from the Home Affairs Select Committee which looked, *en passant*, at prison privatization in 1987. We mentioned earlier that Select Committees had been set up to prise open the closed Whitehall policy making machine of the 1950s and 1960s, to give backbenchers from all parties, and other interested members of the public and the press, a chance to scrutinize the assumptions that underpinned government policies and to make some assessment about the quality of the government's performance in delivering on these policies. It was in the course of a more general inquiry into the state and use of the prison estate that the Committee's chairman, to the genuine surprise of Labour members of the Committee, decided to visit America to inspect and report back on private prisons.

When the hotly contested report was eventually published, it recommended that the government should go ahead and experiment with two privately run remand prisons. It was shown to have been skilfully drafted to conceal that the Committee had only visited one private, adult American prison, and that it had ignored available evidence from academic and US government sources, relying instead almost entirely on the opinions the of CCA, hardly an independent source about the virtues of private prisons.

Given this bias it was not surprising that one Conse
Committee found American private prisons "stunnin,
Conservatives on the Select Committee were not so
Stansbook was unconvinced, and John Hunt was anxious,
should be looked at very carefully indeed before any fina
Labour members of the Committee were *unanimously* agaii
experiment.

In pointing to this pro-privatization lobby my intention ... to stress how the
Conservative Party at this time was all but encapsulated in its own New Right
rhetoric. The suggestion that a quasi-market should be created, that the private
and public sectors should compete for the delivery of punishment, that this
would result in real benefits for all the stakeholders in the system, including
prisoners, was taken as an ideological certainty. That there was no available,
reliable evidence to support this claim was an inconvenience that could be
brushed aside. Not even the delivery of punishment, long regarded as one of the
distinguishing monopolies of modern industrial states, could escape
privatization. Indeed, this apparent uniqueness almost certainly *added to its appeal*
as an ideological target, as some of its advocates have since admitted
(Windlesham 1993)

Old Labour rhetoric

It the light of such obviously partisan rhetoric the Home Secretary's initial
caution was surely understandable. However, it is arguable that the Home
Secretary, his senior civil servants and the traditional penal lobby were caught
up in their own partisan rhetoric—embraced enthusiastically by Labour—which
stubbornly locked them into a tradition which had been endorsed by a previous
Parliamentary committee. This had arbitrated, as long ago as 1810, between the
commercial approach to running the prison system advocated by Bentham and
the State controlled, bureaucratic and moral reformation favoured by G O Paul.
About this arbitration Michael Ignatieff has written:

> In place of a Benthamite conception of authority regulated by market incentives,
> reformers like Paul succeeded in vindicating a bureaucratic formalism that looked to
> inspection and rules as the means to protect inmates against cruelty and to guarantee
> the rigour of punishment. For opponents of the contact system, punishment was too
> delicate a function to be left to private entrepreneurs. For state power to preserve its
> legitimacy, it was essential that it remain untainted with the stain of commerce.

(Ignatieff 1978, p 133)

The triumph of this bureaucratic formalism, enshrined in the later wholesale
nationalization of the prison system in 1877, was deeply ingrained on the Home
Office and the penal lobby, so much so that attempts to defend it were
sometimes either ill informed or muddled, sometimes a mixture of both.

Take, for example, the claim by J E Thomas that the proposal for private
prisons represented a return to the eighteenth century (*The Independent*, July 28
1987). The gaoler then was a public official who secured his income by charging
for services he provided for those prisoners in his care. Under this arrangement
he could therefore do as little or as much as he pleased. His sometimes

practices were not of much concern to the magistrates or sheriffs
...inally oversaw his activities because he made no charge on the public
. This system was completely at odds with the system being proposed in
1980s where private contractors were to be employed under the fairly strict
contractual regulation of the State.

Another critique difficult to sustain was the Howard League's original claim
that the State could not "abdicate" its responsibility for looking after offenders
without undermining the "very essence" of the "liberal democratic" State. If this
was such a danger, then why was the Howard League in much the same breath
willing to endorse the use of private organizations in supervising young
offenders? The fact that these organizations were mostly voluntary rather than
"for profit" was not an issue, or at least, not in terms of the argument advanced
by the league (Ryan and Ward 1989a).

The truth of the matter is that although the prison system had been
nationalized at a stroke in 1877 other parts of the penal system remained and
(developed) in private hands. Reform and industrial schools were a good
example. These had been set up for young people after agitation by Mary
Carpenter in the 1850s. Although no friend of state intervention, always insisting
instead on the virtues of the voluntary sector, Carpenter had been forced to
concede that if these schools were to receive public money they had to accept a
system of certification and regulation. It is true, of course, that some of these
voluntary sector schools used their "pupils" as a form of forced labour and kept
many imprisoned long after they were legally entitled to—problems which the
State wrestled with until well into the twentieth century. But their existence,
however imperfect, is evidence enough that they did not constitute a serious
threat to the principles on which the "liberal democratic" State was being built.

If the example of voluntary industrial and reform schools seems a little
distant, consider something closer to home and far more topical: immigrant
detention centres. In the 1960s these centres, then only at Heathrow and Gatwick,
were the direct responsibility of the Home Office, but their running was
contracted out by a Labour government to Securicor in 1970. In the 1980s there
was much criticism of these centres, it is true. Their officers were said to have
been poorly trained and when a temporary floating centre, *The Earl William*, cut
adrift in a storm in 1988 even more public attention was focussed on their
inadequacies. However, the point I simply wish to make here is that people were
being imprisoned, detained if this sounds easier, and guarded by the private
sector under agreements sanctioned by the Labour Party long before prison
privatization became an issue.

Ideological and political obfuscation also prevented a sensible discussion of
some other key issues. For instance, the argument the penal reform lobby seemed
to be feeling its way towards, namely, that the exercise of deadly force, which
was bound to arise at some time in the *delivery* of punishment at the hard end of
the system, could not be legitimately delegated to private interests, was
sometimes presented as if the State was being encouraged to give up its role in
the *allocation of* punishment. This was never seriously suggested in Britain,
though it was by some far right libertarians in America (Rothbard 1978).

As for the *delivery* of punishment, the uncomfortable truth for opponents of
prison privatization was that while the State alone can define what is legitimate

punishment, it does not necessarily have to trust this to public bodies. Another key issue was profit. That is to say, while it might have seemed wrong at first sight to make money out of the unfortunate necessity of inflicting pain, surely private companies had been building prisons at a considerable profit to themselves and their shareholders for over a century? What could possibly be wrong, in principle, with allowing such companies to make a profit out of running the prisons they had previously built? Was the argument that it might increase the number of prison places available, thus increasing the quantum of pain that any society has at its disposal?

It would have been reasonable to have thought through some of the differences we have outlined here. To have accepted, for example, that the debate about who should guard immigrant detainees *might* raise different issues from those that arise over who should be entrusted to guard prisoners; or to have at least *listened* to the arguments of those who believed that remand prisoners could be looked after by different people from those who guarded convicted prisoners.

But the lobby against privatization was slow to engage with these differences, to acknowledge that the relationship between the State and the penal system was a more complex one than was generally acknowledged; that it was, and continues to be, a fluid one.

This simple truth was lost in the colliding rhetoric of the New Right and old Labour. The traditional lobby had some difficulty in re-positioning itself in the wake of this collision. This led to some strange alliances, for example, with Labour and the Prison Officers' Association standing together having fallen out bitterly in the 1970s (Ryan and Ward 1989). This alliance did have some progressive possibilities, it is true, but it was nonetheless a strange one which others noted at the time (Harding 1994).

In this section I have not sought to explore the arguments for and against prison privatization in any systematic form. I have done that elsewhere (Ryan and Ward 1989). Instead, what I have tried to illustrate is just how fiercely, and sometimes blindly, this audacious new policy was fought over by the New Right and old Labour. I now turn to examine just how the New Right secured its victory.

Securing the victory

The boisterous campaign by lobby groups like the Howard League, the Prison Reform Trust and NACRO in tandem with Labour and the POA enabled a cautious Home Secretary and sceptical civil servants to avoid taking any decision on private prisons for nearly two years. It was, therefore, not until March 1989 that Douglas Hurd announced his *volte face*, telling Parliament that:

> the introduction of the private sector into the management of the prison system would certainly represent a bold departure. It offers the prospect of a new kind of partnership between the public and the private sector in this important ... aspect of our national life. We should not be scornful of new ideas which, if successful, will make an important contribution to the government's programme of providing decent conditions for all prisoners at a reasonable cost.

(*Hansard*, col. 278, 1 March 1989)

The micro-politics behind securing this rupture with past practice are highly instructive. We already know that New Right think tanks and the Home Affairs Select Committee had been lobbying for private prisons, but another senior member of the Home Office team, Lord Windlesham, had also written to the Prime Minister in July 1987 suggesting an experiment with private remand prisons, alongside the privatization of prison escort services. He received a surprisingly cautious reply. Mrs Thatcher suggested that:

> There would be legal problems, and problems to do with accountability, that have not yet been fully explored. At present the balance of the argument seems to be against moving in this direction, and that is why Douglas Hurd told the House of Commons that he did not believe there was a case for handing over the business of keeping prisoners safe to anyone other than Government servants.
>
> As to your specific suggestion that escort arrangements should be privatized, last year the Court Escort Scrutiny Report concluded that the use of private guards for escorting purposes would not be desirable since it would only further complicate an already complex system. It recommended instead that after implementation of the other recommendations, consideration should be given to the creation of a special grade of escort officer.
>
> (Quoted in Windlesham 1993, pp 278/9)

This was cautious, not to say discouraging, and for some months cast a shadow over the prospects for prison and escort service privatization. However, two key developments were to change government thinking radically. The first was a visit by the Home Office Minister responsible for prisons, the Earl of Caithness, to inspect private prisons in America. His report was highly favourable, and this had a considerable impact (Faulkner, Oxford 2000). Second, senior Conservative members of the Select Committee conducted a skilful Parliamentary campaign to keep the issue alive and before the public, while lobby groups arranged private meetings at venues like the Carlton Club (October 1988) and, with the help and support of the Adam Smith Institute, held seminars bringing together commercial and party interests. Lord Windlesham gives us the power and flavour of this lobby:

> The overlap between Party political and commercial interest was exemplified by the attendance at a seminar held over dinner held at the Carlton Club ... The event was organized as one of a series by the Club's Political Committee ...
>
> The private sector was out in strength. As well as the new consortia, representatives of other construction businesses were present, together with all the principal security firms. One of CCA's rivals from the United States also sent a representative. After the seminar, a detailed policy paper was drafted and circulated ... Copies were sent to the relevant ministers and their special advisors, the Cabinet Office and the Policy Unit at 10 Downing Street.
>
> (Windlesham 1993, p 289)

The confidence this suggests partly reflected the tone of a Green Paper that had been published a few months earlier, *Private Sector Involvement in the Remand System* (Cm 434 HMSO London 1988). This claimed that many of the problems associated with maintaining standards in prisons and securing their accountability had already been resolved, in America at least, so there should be no problems in the United Kingdom, even though our legal and constitutional framework was somewhat different.

Little or no evidence was provided for this claim about the American experience; it was little more than a highly contentious assertion. However, it set the tone for the rest of the document which one leading member of the pro-privatization lobby later described as a White Paper with green borders! (Ryan and Ward 1989). In other words, the government had more or less made up its mind. Privatizing escort services was also supported in the Green Paper.

Interestingly, however, Hurd's successor, David Waddington, was even less inclined to introduce private interests into the prison system. It was only with the intervention of Mrs Thatcher that Whitehall's inertia was overcome and provision for private remand prisons written into the Criminal Justice Bill (1991). The Bill was then controversially amended at the Report stage in Parliament, giving the Home Secretary powers to authorize any private prison, and not just those operating in the remand sector. This late change took the Opposition completely by surprise.

Mrs Thatcher's role here, as elsewhere, was pivotal in securing change. As Lord Windlesham puts it, she was:

> the ideologically convinced outsider, temperamentally opposed to vested interest, producer dominance, and the monopoly of labour in the public sector as in the private.
>
> Discordant as were the arguments advanced by the Adam Smith Institute and the other free market proselytizers with received opinion in most Whitehall Departments, nevertheless they were often a truer articulation of the political beliefs of the occupant of 10 Downing Street than the decisions of ministers in whom Mrs Thatcher not infrequently detected signs of having been brainwashed by the bureaucracy over which she expected them to take charge.
>
> (Windlesham 1993, p 298)

Nothing better links the wider politics of the New Right to prison privatization than this insider observation. The rupture in Prison Service delivery was ideologically driven from the top. Resistance had been overcome. By 1991 legislation was in place providing for the creation of a quasi-market in line with the dictates of the new institutional economics.

Civil Service resistance

Lord Windlesham's strongly implied criticism of the Civil Service, and it was shared by many Conservatives at the time, needs to be considered at two levels.

At a general level, it was argued that senior civil servants, not least in the Home Office, acquired great administrative expertise and were at work in their departments for much longer than ministers who came and went after only a year or two. This continuity gave them great power. It is difficult, as Labour politicians found in the 1960s, to shift them, not least when what ministers propose runs contrary to departmental policies that had been tried and tested. This was reinforced by an *esprit de corps* among the higher Civil Service that came from a shared training, often shared social values, and perhaps above all else, a commitment to the ideals of public service. The fact that they were permanent, that they had job security, gave them even greater scope to frustrate their political masters, not least when it came to reforming the service itself, as we have already noted.

Against this background it is hardly surprising that there was Civil Service resistance to the policies of the New Right. Its programme not only rejected many well established departmental policies, but also suggested that the top down, hierarchical model of delivering public services should be pretty much dismantled and replaced, either by wholesale privatization, as in the cases of the great public utilities, or by delivering other services, including some welfare services, through the market place. Mrs Thatcher had difficulty in securing this revolution. She could not always find what she called "can do" civil servants who were enthusiastic and willing to think laterally and create markets for delivering health, education, or even, punishment. As a result of this inertia, there were attempts to bring people from the private sector into the Civil Service on short term contracts and even, at one point, to replace a whole phalanx of senior civil servants (Maor 1999).

How did this resistance manifest itself in the Home Office? I think the first point to acknowledge is that there *was* resistance, at all levels. Windlesham is correct to imply this, though it also has to be said that once the green light was given there was much dedicated effort by middle ranking civil servants to make privatization work. This was particularly true in the Remands Unit, though even here the tension between public and private was starkly drawn when a member of the unit involved in contracting out left to work for the private sector. This move became the subject of an internal Civil Service inquiry. Clearly, however, of far more significance was the attitude of the senior civil servants in the Home Office.

My own reading of their position is that privatization was unwelcome, though perhaps not for the obvious reasons. Let me put it this way. Given the department's evidence to the May Inquiry about the virtues of public service, it might be thought that senior civil servants were simply out to maintain the *status quo*. It is not entirely unreasonable to interpret their resistance in this way. It also has to be admitted that some senior civil servants were sceptical about private prisons because they believed there were too few players in the market place to generate effective competition. However, my own view is that what really dictated senior Civil Service opposition, indifference might be a better word, was the belief that prison privatization was largely irrelevant.

The context was simply this. The Home Office had been preparing for the introduction of what was to become the Criminal Justice Act 1991 for several years. Its strategic priority was to cap the escalating prison population by introducing new sentencing principles and to develop more alternatives to custody, to make them more acceptable to the judiciary and the public. Senior civil servant David Faulkner travelled thousands of miles and gave dozens of speeches trying to mobilize consent for this Home Office policy that Douglas Hurd fully supported (Rutherford 1996). It was no easy task. The Probation Service, for example, was wary of the toughening up and centralizing tendencies that this policy implied, and senior judges had to be persuaded that it did not involve any encroachment on judicial independence. Getting the higher judiciary on board proved to be a delicate business (Faulkner, Oxford 2000). Then there was the penal lobby to persuade.

It was right in the middle of this difficult (and cherished) project that prison privatization surfaced. Senior civil servants considered it. They were not enthralled by it, perhaps partly because it undermined their stewardship of the prison system, perhaps even because they had a liberal distaste for commercialism, but most of all they thought it largely irrelevant to solving the wider problems of the criminal justice system which they intended the 1991 Act to address. This produced inertia, mostly, but also some irritation.

But of course, if the government wanted prison privatization then the Civil Service knew it must have it, properly thought out, and starting as an experiment. That the 1991 Act provided for the use of private prisons across the system as a whole without any proper evaluation, is likely to have dismayed senior civil servants, as it did Labour, and even it has to be acknowledged, Lord Windlesham. But by then there was no modifying the process, the battle had been well and truly lost.

THE SPREAD OF PRIVATIZATION

The subsequent growth of privatization was somewhat uneven. The first privately managed prison in Britain for over 100 years was opened at HMP The Wolds in Lincolnshire in 1992. This had been financed by the public sector and was intended to house 300 prisoners awaiting trial or sentence. The builders were UK Detention Contractors, a consortium of two leading UK construction firms, Mowlem and McAlpine, with the Corrections Corporation of America as consultants. The contract to manage the prison went to Group 4, a private security firm that had previously managed immigrant detention centres.

Right from the beginning HMP The Wolds was subject to immense media and union scrutiny, much of it highly critical. But apart from this attention, HMP The Wolds, like any other prison, was subject to an inspection by HM Chief Inspector of Prisons who found that while prisoners were treated with courtesy, they were provided with little purposeful activity once outside of their cells, and that a bail information scheme which had been specified in the original contract had not been set up. More controversial, however, was the availability of drugs, including alcohol. Security was very lax on this front and the Chief Inspector recommended that the so-called "drugs free" unit be closed down at once.

These criticisms, and it has to be said that the governor, Stephen Twinn, came out of the inspection less damaged than many other governors in charge of State managed prisons at that time, did not deter the government from opening a second privately managed prison, Blakenhurst, this time to house around 650 sentenced and unsentenced prisoners. The contract to run HMP Blakenhurst was given to United Kingdom Detention Services (UKDS), a consortium headed by the Corrections Corporation of America and supported by building contractors Mowlem and McAlpine. The general manager of the HMP Blakenhurst project was American and staff from HMP Blakenhurst went to America for training.

By the mid-1990s two other State financed prisons had been contracted out to the private sector to manage, HMPs Doncaster and Buckley Hall, holding 850 and 300 prisoners respectively. By this time there were around 2,000 prisoners being managed by the private sector. However, it was not until the second half of the 1990s that the government signed contracts with the private sector to fund, design, build and manage two new private prisons. These contracts were awarded for 20 years and their capital value at the time was estimated to be around £100 million. HMP Fazakerley was scheduled to hold 600 prisoners and HMP Bridgend 800 prisoners. The government also announced that a further 12 privately built prisons would come on stream after 2000 (PRT, June 1996). The target around this time was to have the private sector managing/owning approximately ten to 15 per cent of the total prison estate.

The government's attempt to involve the private sector in taking over the management of *existing* State managed prisons ran into the European Business Transfer Directive (TUPE) in 1992. What this EC directive requires is that the existing pay and conditions, including pension rights, of public service employees must be guaranteed if their enterprises transfer from the public to the private sector. This makes State prisons much less attractive to the private sector, and so far the only market tested prison, HMP Strangeways, which was partially rebuilt following the massive disturbances there in 1990, went to an "in house" bid, which surprised no one. The Prison Service was not allowed to enter a bid to run new prisons at that time.

The pace of privatization was faster in some other, arguably less contentious service areas, such as prison catering. But even more dramatic, the private sector quickly moved to take over court and prison escort services throughout the country with Group 4 Court Services and Premier Prison Services taking the lead. The credibility of the private sector in this area was seriously dented when prisoners were inexplicably lost. For some months Group 4 became a metaphor for managerial inefficiency and incompetence. One tabloid newspaper, the *Sun,* offered its readers £20 for every Group 4 joke they published. This humour took a sour note when Ernest Hogg died while being transported from HMP The Wolds to court, nor was he the last prisoner to die in the care of the private sector (Ryan 1993). A coroner's jury also decided that Alton Manning, a 33-year-old black remand prisoner had been unlawfully killed at HMP Blakenhurst in December 1996 (PRT, April 1998).

The overall performance of the private sector is not my main concern here, though I think it is fairly obvious that it did not always reach the standards of excellence that its advocates so glibly promised it would, but the catastrophe that some of its detractors predicted did not happen either. (For an even handed evaluation of two comparable prisons operating at this time, one in the public sector, the other private, see James *et al.* 1997). What this sketch does demonstrate, however, is that by the end of the 1990s the private prisons were pretty much a fixture.[2]

While most prisons at this time remained, and indeed, still remain in the public sector, the use of the private sector fractured the penal landscape.

What had once been a highly centralized, unified public service in which every detail surrounding the daily routine of prisoners, and those who guarded and transported them, was set down at the centre was now a binary system with

---

[2] There are currently ten private prisons in England and Wales operated by four separate companies (*Howard League Magazine*, vol. 2. no. 2, May 2002). The performance of Premier Prison Services Ltd at Ashfield YOI has been subject to much criticism, and its director there was replaced by the Director General of HM Prison Service with a prison service governor using emergency powers in the Criminal Justice Act 1991 which had provided for the introduction of private prisons.

different pay and conditions for public and private sector employees, while "stimulus" of competition and profit lay at the interface between them. Furthermore, while both public and private sector prisons remained accountable to the centre, their day-to-day operations were placed further from direct political accountability when in 1993 the Prison Department at the Home Office was hived off and given agency status under the government's Next Steps programme. The new Director General of the Prison Service ceased to be a career civil servant, and instead was recruited directly from the private sector.

The impact of privatization on the level of the prison population

One of the many fears of those who opposed prison privatization was that its introduction might lead to an overall increase in the prison population. This fear rested on a simple logic. Private corporations might lobby for more offenders to be sent to prison; this would stimulate the demand for more private prisons, thus offering shareholders the potential for even greater profits. Given the demonstrated political and economic clout of the companies then involved, the potential power of this penal industrial complex was no *mirage*.

However, Britain's biggest prison building programme since Victorian times had been announced in the early 1980s, long before the issue of privatization surfaced. To be sure, it could be argued that the penal industrial complex was well placed to have encouraged this expansion. Mowlem and McAlpine, for example, made regular financial contributions to the Conservative Party. But even if this were to be proved, it cannot plausibly be argued that prison privatization was the *motor* of prison expansion in the 1980s and 1990s, that it drove it. If anything, the motor for this expansion, as we shall see in *Part IV*, was a combination of wider ideological, political and social factors that encouraged more robust policing and tougher sentencing in the face of industrial disruption and urban unrest. These factors had little to do with the power of the penal industrial complex.

The truth of the matter is that sentencing policy is many layered, driven by a multitude of forces that are likely to vary across time and space. So, for example, a complex analysis would be required to understand the forces responsible for driving up prison populations in America and in some Australian states in the 1990s. The fact that private prisons were operating in both these jurisdictions may have been of no more significance there than it was in Britain. What might have been pivotal instead, for example, was the "war on drugs".

However, if this fear of direct intervention by the penal industrial complex was over drawn at the time in Britain, there is another context in which it *was* to become meaningful and this should be discernible from what we already know, namely, the New Right's determination to reduce public expenditure and public borrowing. The private sector's offer to finance, as well as to design, build and then manage new prisons became a very attractive proposition in the 1990s under a variety of initiatives, first as the Private Finance Initiative (PFI) and then later as Public, Private Partnerships (PPP). Arrangements like these enabled governments to spread their capital expenditure over a long period. And what could be wrong with the private sector picking up the initial tab for funding private prisons?

…te sector could fund and build hospitals why not prisons? In this …l industrial complex facilitated the expansion of the prison system. And …ion New Labour came to accept.

NEW LABOUR PRACTICE EMBRACES NEW PUBLIC MANAGEMENT

The first element of the New Public Management (NPM) programme which we referred to above as the new institutional economics was thus in place by the mid-1990s: a quasi-market had been established by the Conservatives and the prison system had been cut adrift from its stifling, bureaucratic centre.

For a while Labour continued to oppose prison privatization root and branch. It had argued that like most people it believed that delivering punishment should only be entrusted to the State. During the 1997 General Election campaign shadow Home Secretary Jack Straw said on BBC radio that Labour would sign no more contracts for new private prisons and, "within the existing budget, [we] shall take back into the public service privatized prisons as soon as contractually possible" (PRT, May 1997). This reinforced a statement he had made to the Prison Officers' Association a little earlier that he had "a fundamental objection to prisons run by the private sector" (*Gatelodge*, April 1997). Shortly after the 1997 General Election, however, Straw indicated a shift in the government's thinking, arguing that: "if there are contracts in the pipeline, and the only way of getting the [new prison] accommodation in place very quickly is by signing those contracts, then I will sign those contracts" (PRT, May 1997).

Everyone in the penal lobby knew long before the General Election that the only way to get new accommodation "quickly" was to use the private sector, everyone except Mr Straw, apparently. (Straw's later decision to take HMP Buckley Hall back into the State sector was a surprise, but it did not signal a retreat from the government's commitment to private prisons.)[2]

If this sounds too cynical, I think the distance New Labour had travelled is perhaps best illustrated by the Home Affairs Select Committee which reported at about the same time, in March 1997, on *The Management of the Prison Service; Public and Private* (HMSO 1997). In that report para 202 emphasized that *"there needs to be a continued expansion of the private sector if the full benefits of competition are to be maintained"*. This was the only issue on which the Committee divided, and there was only one dissenting voice, old Labour's Gerry Bermingham. He had served on the controversial Home Affairs Select Committee that had examined the case for private prisons a decade earlier (see above).

Other New Labour members of the Committee lined up with the Conservatives, and this was hardly surprising. After all, New Labour had by then jettisoned Clause 4, embraced the market, announced already that it would not contest the large scale privatizations undertaken by the Conservatives since 1979 and, with a few caveats, embraced the re-modelling of the Welfare State to

---

[2] Nor does the return of HMP Blakenhurst to the state sector (*Howard League Magazine*, vol. 2. no. 2, May 2002).

improve efficiency by distancing the State from the day-to-day management of delivering its services.

Furthermore, in order to make this downward thrust of government possible, New Labour enthusiastically took on board the second element of the NPM: the use of a whole range of standards and measures of performance borrowed from the private sector by which not only are individuals within an agency judged, but agencies themselves can be audited from the centre. In doing this, New Labour accepted that these agencies had to have a degree of transparency built into them to make evaluation through audit possible. Without this the State was and still is unwilling to let go, to loosen its governance.

For instance, setting Key Performance Indicators (KPIs) for those delivering services, and then auditing them to assess performance, is one of the techniques that makes the disaggregation of government possible; without them, or something like them, value for money would be impossible to judge. But more than just this, without such mechanisms in place governments would have no means of evaluating their success in meeting their strategic objectives, and so these must be increasingly refined and made explicit in order to make measurement through audit possible.

To give some flavour of how these mechanisms worked, the Prisons Agency was audited around the number of prison escapes, the number of assaults on prison staff, the number of hours that prisoners spent out of their cells and so forth. Having to work to these KPIs was thought to have contributed more than any other single factor, more even, presumably, than the introduction of private prisons, to the improvement in the agency's performance in the 1990s. The Director General of the agency was quite triumphant about this in evidence to the 1996/7 Select Committee:

> It is irrefutable that our performance has improved enormously over this period. I think the biggest contributor has been the establishing of key performance indicators and targets. That has focussed people's attention on improving performance.
>
> (HMSO 1997, vol. 11, para 133; James *et al.* 1997)

By the time this Committee had reported, strongly endorsing privatization and the new managerialism in the prison system, the New Right's agenda had become the centre ground of political debate. Gerry Bermingham MP had been overtaken by events. Had no one told him that the Berlin Wall had come down, and that markets now ruled?

An explanatory note on audit
The audit function of government, which has been so instrumental in securing many of the changes I have been describing, is often explained in very technical language. I want to explain this function in plainer language, as best I can, so that we can better understand its *political* content.

Some basics
Accountability for the use of public money is the cornerstone of democratic government. As citizens we need to know what sums of money have been voted by our representatives to be spent by this or that department or service, and then,

fairly obviously, we need an audit to make sure that the monies have been spent on the things that Parliament said they should be spent on.

In Britain this work is done by the Comptroller and Auditor General as head of the National Audit Office which was set up in its present form in 1983. The Auditor General and his or her army of accountants audit the great departments of State like the Home Office and Next Steps Agencies like the Prison Service Agency. However, a lot of budgets voted by Parliament get spent locally or by authorities that are neither central government departments nor agencies, for example local authorities or the NHS. These accounts are mostly audited by the Comptroller through the Audit Commission which was also established by statute in 1983. Given the scale of government audit, work is regularly contracted out to professional firms in the private sector.

The fact that these new audit arrangements were put in place by the New Right is, of course, significant, but this should not be overstated since governments of all political persuasions have shown an increasing interest in audit. This is not just for the sake of probity, to make sure that the money voted by Parliament has been spent on what it was intended for, and within the limits set. Instead, audits are increasingly carried out under the banner of economy, efficiency and effectiveness. Value for Money (VFM) has, therefore, long been the auditor's main concern rather than "candle ends" accounting, to borrow a Gladstonian term. So, in recent years the Audit Commission has carried out a large number of VFM audits in the criminal justice system, into the Court Service (focusing on the Crown Court) and the provincial police forces, for example.

Of course, any audit which goes beyond mere accounting has to recognize any agencies' or services' strategically defined objectives, and what is more, will need to see what mechanisms those organizations have in place to measure whether these objectives are being met, such as Key Performance Indicators. These mechanisms are now regarded as essential.

Indeed, the auditor's modern role is more to see that these mechanisms are in place, that any organization it investigates has built into its structure and operations mechanisms *to police itself*, rather than to simply report that this or that KPI was not met. (It does not take a good deal of insight to see that the Probation and Aftercare Service of the 1980s with its local practices and disagreements over its functions was ripe for the modern auditor's attention, which it duly got!)

It is also clear that audit interacts with politics to a high degree in the sense that strategic objectives are inevitably refined in the process of setting up and then carrying out an audit. Auditors press politicians and their civil servants. What are the strategic objectives? Have the objectives been prioritized? In other words, what is to be measured? Is the work of the agency organized in such a way that its performance in working towards these strategic objectives can be measured?

It is also significant that because of its wide ranging scope the Audit Commission is well placed to make comparisons about the quality of public service delivery across government, and to suggest where "best practice" might be shared. The Commission's ability to employ auditors from the private sector has also enabled it to make comparisons between public and private sector practice, and to draw on "best practice" from across the board. This overview has made the Commission particularly well placed to oversee the quality of the ever-increasing amount of inter-agency work being undertaken, particularly at local levels in the criminal justice system.

Youth justice

A recent example of this at work was the 1999 Audit Commission inquiry into the implementation of the Crime and Disorder Act 1998 which was partly about speeding up the youth justice service. The Commission's updated report, *Misspent Youth '99: The Challenge for Youth Justice* (HMSO 1999), found that significant progress had been made. The average time between arrest and sentence in the youth court in 1998 was 102 days for all offenders and 103 days for "persistent offenders". This was a considerable reduction of the previous year's figures. However, the report went on to demonstrate that there were still significant variations in the time between arrest and sentence—in some youth courts it was 50 days, in others, 189 days. Clearly there were lessons to be learnt, benchmarks for service delivery to be set out and best practice identified.

While the Audit Commission can make its own decisions about what VFM audits it undertakes, these are often the outcome of negotiations with government. Increasingly, therefore, audit is seen as a tool of government, and not unreasonably so, one might think.

The danger, however, is that in such audits, which depend on evaluating strategically defined, political objectives, the Commission might overstep its authority and encroach upon what is essentially political territory. This charge has been convincingly made about its earlier audit of youth justice, *Misspent Youth: Young People and Crime* (HMSO 1996), and also its audit of regional policing (Raine and James 1998). In the former, for example, the Commission argued that the huge sums spent on processing a relatively small number of offenders through the courts would be better spent on preventative services. This implied a policy shift from justice to welfare; resource management was here being used to dictate policy. This blurring of the political and the administrative is further illustrated by the fact that these recommendations found favour with New Labour in Opposition and a member of the audit team later joined the Home Office as one of Jack Straw's key policy advisors shortly after the 1997 General Election (Raine and James 1998).

It would be glib to suggest that "auditors now rule". Their increasing influence, however, is surely not in doubt. This was made abundantly clear in the debate about reinstating the Advisory Council on the Penal System which followed the return of New Labour in 1997. The government refused to resurrect the Council, pointing out, again not unreasonably perhaps, that the range of policy advice available to ministers is now far greater than it was in the cosy 1950s and 1960s. There has been the creation of independent inspectorates for prisons and probation, advice from the Criminal Justice Consultative Council recommended by the Woolf inquiry and reports from democratically accountable Select Committees, like the Home Affairs Select Committee which played such a key role in the debate about privatization. However, included very prominently in the list of new advisors were auditors.

We now have input from the National Audit Office and the Audit Commission, both of which have a role to play in advising on efficiency and effectiveness on these matters—for example ....

The Audit Commission's report on youth justice was a seminal work, and informed the provisions in the Bill to reform practice and legislation.

(*Hansard*, Standing Committee B, col. 12, 28 April 1998)

The Audit Commission's work on agreeing partnership indicators between local authorities and ACPO was also given a special mention.

Audit might not have exclusive rights of access, but it now definitely has the inside track, constituting, one might almost say, a new and increasingly powerful force in an increasingly complex policy making network. Auditors are among the new experts. They may not rule, but their "grey science", their knowledge, has become increasingly influential over and against the human sciences which once sat at the top table.

POLITICAL CONTROL

The changes outlined in this essay represented a significant re-modelling of the State apparatus, greatly altering the style of government I outlined in *Part I*. Large areas of government activity covering the public utilities have been hived off, along with their civil servants, under a variety of regulatory mechanisms, and agencies have been introduced to facilitate markets and the evaluation of service delivery transformed. The pattern and extent of change has been summarized by Rhodes who goes so far as to argue that:

Since 1945 the institutions of British government have experienced two revolutions. The postwar Labour government built the Welfare State and its institutions but these have barely survived three decades before a reforming Conservative government sought to redefine and abolish many.

(Rhodes 1997, p 5)

The sheer extent of this transformation has led to the suggestion that top down central government is no longer the reality; that there is no longer even a governing political authority at the centre, but instead a "multiplicity of actors specific to each policy area", increasing "interdependence" among policy makers and administrators and a blurring of boundaries between public, private and voluntary actors" (Rhodes 1997, p 51). While many of these trends can be identified in the changes I have outlined in the prison system, not least with the recent encouragement of more voluntary sector "partnerships" with prisons (PRT 2000), such a complete post-modern description, the suggestion that we live in a "centreless society" (Luhmann 1982, p 253) is surely a contentious, not to say misleading, one .

In the first place, it can *imply* that the new governance is less about exerting central control than it once was, when in truth the new mechanisms are about doing exactly the *opposite*, they represent a new and more intensive technology of control. As Nicolas Rose puts it:

Neo-liberalism does not abandon "the will to govern", it maintains the view that failure of government to achieve its objectives is to be overcome by inventing new strategies of government that will succeed ...

(Rose 1996, p 53)

Second, the new mechanisms of disaggregation do not always work smoothly, but collide with older traditions of accountability. To explore this point I wish to briefly focus on the question of ministerial responsibility and the public controversy that surrounded the dismissal of the first Director General of the Prison Service Agency, Derek Lewis.

The creation of such agencies carries with it both the explicit and implicit desire of overloaded government to separate out the policy making functions of government from operational concerns. The intention of handing over the "murky plain of overwhelming detail" to managers is clear (Power 1997). So in the case of the Prison Service Agency, Derek Lewis was to have control over the day-to-day operation of the Prison Service, to revolutionize its complex tasks in line with private sector practices as we described above, while the Home Secretary would be in charge of policy (HMSO 1993). In order to indicate the significance of this change Parliamentary questions addressed to the Home Secretary about the day-to-day running of the Prison Service were printed in *Hansard* as replies from the Director General. There was to be an end to the silly pretence that home secretaries actually *managed* the Prison Service in a "hands-on" manner.

This division of responsibilities worked somewhat unevenly for a while, but finally broke down altogether over the dismissal of John Marriott, the governor of Parkhurst prison, where there had been a serious security lapse. While this was under investigation, Derek Lewis had decided to move the governor, a decision that was clearly his under the service's Code of Discipline, but he was overruled by the Home Secretary of the day, Michael Howard, who insisted that Marriott be sacked.

It has to be said that this episode was the culmination of a long period of "interference" by government that showed an unhealthy interest in the "murky" day-to-day detail of the Prison Service, not least when it appeared to contradict policy. So, for example, Michael Howard's famous announcement that prison regimes should be more "austere" appeared, at least tacitly, to be undermined by the operational decision of the Director General to allow televisions in prison cells. In the end, Derek Lewis was sacked in what became a *cause célèbre*. (For a thoughtful comparison between the prisons and special secure hospitals under Next Steps, see Kaye 1998.)

What is interesting about this episode for us is that while those who write about a "revolution in governance" are right to suggest that the Prison Service now interfaces between public and private, including an increasing number of voluntary actors; that there is indeed a growing interdependence between both political and administrative actors, it is surely premature to imply that the centre has collapsed. Indeed, one might even argue, particularly if we take into account the increasing control that private sector contracts give to the centre and the new audit processes that are in place, that governments have *increased* their power over the penal apparatus (Clarke J, Cochrane A and Maclaughin E 1994). As if to confirm this, Jack Straw, reinstated the *status quo ante* in 1997 and now all Parliamentary answers about prison matters have the Home Secretary's imprint.

The Probation and Aftercare Service

It is also clear that government has consolidated its control over the Probation and Aftercare Service. This is relevant here because it illustrates that the starting point for those post-modernists who place the desegregation of government at the centre of their analysis, as opposed shall we say, to the introduction of the new managerialism, are inclined to write as if the postwar revolution in government immediately swept every social service into the arms of the State where they have waited patiently ever since for their "liberation".

The history of the Probation and Aftercare Service suggests quite the opposite experience. We have already seen that the service became more regulated as a result of the Criminal Justice Act 1948. But it still remained an essentially small, local service serving 292 independent local areas. However, as the role of the service expanded in the 1960s and 1970s to include things like prison aftercare, its numbers grew, increasing by 3,553 to 5,168 between 1960 and 1978. This growth was accompanied by more centralization, so by 1995 there were a mere 56 local probation areas, and the government's financial contribution to maintaining the service increased from 50 per cent to 80 per cent (May 1995, p 19).

This concentration obviously enhanced the Home Office's capacity to manage (or guide) the service. Even so, as I demonstrated in *Part II*, rank and file probation officers still exercized enough local autonomy in the 1970s to frustrate the ambitions of Whitehall. But this independence was becoming more and more tenuous, and in 1985 the Home Office for the first time issued a Statement of National Objectives (SNOP) for discussion and comment within the service (Statham and Whitehead 1992)

True, these were vigorously contested by NAPO, and while the need for some local variations was accepted in principle, it was becoming increasingly obvious that central government was determined to exercise greater control. For example, in response to its demands for the service to deliver increasingly more intrusive alternatives to custody to relieve the growing pressure on the prison system, government was clearly unhappy with the amount of time some local services spent on civil work. It was partly the failure to agree these strategic priorities that, understandably and inevitably, made the Audit Commission's recommendations that the Home Office establish Key Performance Indicators for the service as a whole so problematic as Whitehall struggled to respond to the new mantra of economy, efficiency and effectiveness, and later, to implement new financial management systems suggested by the accountants Deloitte, Haskins and Sells (Audit Commission 1989). These were the same accountants who had previously advised the government on the feasibility of private prisons.

Faced with this truculence New Labour decided to further centralize the Probation and Aftercare Service in the bitterly contested Criminal Justice and Court Services Act 2000. This provides for a national Director of Probation to be appointed by the Home Secretary; and the re-organization of the service into 42 probation areas to correspond with local police jurisdictions. The power of appointment to local Probation Boards charged with managing each of the 42 areas lies with the Home Secretary, with the exception of judges who are nominated by the Lord Chancellor. The Home Secretary is to direct local boards about how to discharge their statutory duties, and he can replace them where he believes they are failing in their duty.

Taken together, these changes have transferred the management of a once loosely organized local service into the heart of the modern State apparatus, though interestingly not as an agency. The full extent of this transformation is well captured by civil servant David Faulkner who was directly involved in managing some of these changes until the early 1990s. About the service he writes:

> It had previously thought of itself as a more or less autonomous group of largely independent practitioners, loosely co-ordinated by benevolent principal probation officers and employed by well-intentioned probation committees composed mostly of lay magistrates. It was now to become a managed, criminal justice service, functioning as part of a managed criminal justice system, working in accordance with nationally determined priorities and contributing to the achievement of the government's objectives. (Faulkner 2001, p 312)

The need for an integrated, "whole system" approach was endorsed by the subsequent Halliday report, *Making Punishments Work* (Home Office 2001, p 7).

The fact that this contested change to the structure and role of the Probation Service was secured at all is testimony to the existence of a governing political authority at the centre. The form in which it was secured is testimony to the observable fact that the "revolution in governance" we have witnessed has no singular "disaggregated" form, and indeed, that even where government has been "joined up" into a series of more tightly regulated systems, these systems comprise a variety of constituent parts. Making revolutionary strategies operational rarely produces administrative uniformity.

CONCLUSION

In 1988 I was well advanced in researching a book on private prisons (Ryan and Ward 1989). I guessed that once I had returned from America in the spring of the following year I would be able to sit down with my co-author and put the finishing touches to our manuscript. With this timetable in mind I thought it appropriate to start speaking to publishers and began by telephoning Blackwells in Oxford one Friday afternoon to speak to someone who recently steered through, I was told, a very useful book on alternatives to prison. When I outlined my proposal there was a slight pause, followed by a good natured but enormous chuckle, then the observation that I must be joking. Prison privatization would surely never happen here! I had to look elsewhere for a publisher and fortunately other, academic colleagues with surer political antennae came to the rescue.

I tell this story to embarrass no one, but to illustrate just how audacious the idea of private prisons was to most people. Indeed, even its main proponents at the time, Peter Young at the Adam Smith Institute, once described the idea as being a bit "whacky". Explaining this disbelief is not that difficult.

The prison system had been more thoroughly nationalized than any other public service, more so than education or even Britain's precious health service, and the assumption among those senior civil servants who ran it with great pride was that it would remain a wholly public service, as I have demonstrated. This assumption was shared by just about everyone else in the penal lobby, by Labour and the Prison Officers' Association. The grubby hand of commercialism had been exorcised from the delivery of punishment long ago, the argument was finished. Even those who were prepared to, or, as in the case of senior civil servants, obliged to look at the idea, thought of it as largely irrelevant, that it was something they could sideline while they addressed the real issues that were facing the penal system. But all these restraining interests were outmanoeuvred.

Driven on by the ideological fervour of the New Right the Prison Service was portrayed as yet another public service where producer dominance had generated overly powerful trade unions who ran things to suit themselves rather than accommodate the interests of other stakeholders in the system, taxpayers and even, some argued, prisoners themselves (ASI 1987). *The Times* endorsed this ideological message, openly arguing in its leader columns that privatization should be used to combat the industrial muscle of the POA whose capacity to block prison reform rested on its members being monopoly "providers" offering their services to a single buyer, the government (*The Times*, 21 October 1991; *The Times*, 28 October 1992). Quite how the POA had survived was something of a mystery to *The Times*, as it was to the first Director of the Prisons Agency who was later to write that:

> The POA must have been the last bastion of 1960s trade unionism. I had come to the Prisons Service from the megaphone militancy of trade unionism in the car industry in the 1960s and 70s and the extraordinary feather bedding of the television industry in the 1970s and early 80s ... Whether by accident or design the POA escaped Margaret Thatcher's emasculation of the unions in the 80s.

> (Lewis 1997, p 130)

Some advocates of prison privatization may argue that the policy was about more than simply unleashing market forces to crush the POA. Lord Windlesham, for example, with his particular concern for remand prisoners can reasonably make such a claim, but *significantly* he is the first to admit that what eventually secured prison privatization, getting it over the final hurdle, was its strong ideological appeal. It tuned in with the prevailing *zeitgeist*; in a way, it serves as a powerful ideological index of those times. The penal lobby was changed by the events I have outlined in this essay.

The arrival of the Corrections Corporation of America and Group 4 signalled that the prisons *business* was now *global*. Both companies were to develop significant interests (through subsidiary holdings) in Australia where prison privatization galloped ahead faster than in America or Europe, involving some even larger international corporations, Wakenhut, for example. Those operating British prisons, who lobbied about how these institutions should be funded and managed, now operated beyond the sovereign State. American lobbyists, in that apparently easy, good humoured way that they have, spoke about being on the "chicken run" as they touted for business alongside their public employees.

Equally significant, the discourse of penal reform had to adapt to the language of New Right think tanks like the Adam Smith Institute and Deloitte, Haskins and Sells, the accountants who continued to advise the government on prison privatization and its management. These lobbyists, rather than the Howard League, or even the government funded NACRO, now had the ear of government. Furthermore, we already know that the Advisory Council on the Penal System had not been re-appointed, that instead government departments were busy building new networks with the Audit Commission as it wrestled with the new imperatives of economy, efficiency and effectiveness.

It would not be far from the mark to conclude from this that the narrow, *patrician* world so well evoked by Sir Leon Radzinowicz's *memoire* with its ethos of public service was pretty much dead by the late 1980s; that by then fiscal and administrative calculation had overtaken simple moral calculation. However, I pointed out earlier that an elite policy making *ensemble* continued to exist, if not quite in the old form, throughout the 1980s and into the early 1990s, encompassing the "usual suspects". This carried on debating the direction of penal policy around those powerful, liberal civil servants whom the Director of the Prisons Agency was still criticising in 1997 for running the Home Office as if their responsibilities were "too weighty" to be trusted to transitory politicians! (Lewis 1997)

The 1980s then, was a time when in line with many other government departments, the Home Office was operating in a turbulent administrative environment under the hammer of NPM. It never fully embraced prison privatization, did little to encourage it, eventually responding to it with considerable administrative efficiency, but only when forced to do so by intense political pressure. It learned to sup with the devil, so to speak, to engage with, though not to embrace, Group 4 and the CCA on a routine basis. Some other changes "foisted" on the department were also resented. For example, Sir Clive Whitmore is said to have been unconvinced by arguments for agency status and later avoided clashing with Home Secretary Michael Howard by retiring early. Derek Lewis also recounts enormous scepticism over, and resistance to, some of the private sector management techniques he sought to introduce to improve the operational efficiency of the prison system (Lewis 1977). Throughout all these upheavals, Home Office officials were coming to terms with the growing influence of audit, the government's Financial Management Initiative and trying to bring local government and victims more into the equation.

At the centre of all this senior civil servant David Faulkner held on to the reins of criminal justice policy, orchestrating his own elite *ensemble*, and between 1981 and 1990 delivering 120 speeches and seminar papers across the country to mobilize support for that policy which was geared towards reducing the use of custody within the overall framework of a more integrated criminal justice system. In the middle of this revolution in the machinery of and practice of governance, getting the Criminal Justice Act 1991 onto the statute book was a *bravura* performance and testimony to the enormous skill and influence of the senior Civil Service.

Continuing influence might be a more appropriate phrase. What I wish to suggest here is that while the process of "modernizing the mandarins" did indeed irrevocably change the Civil Service in the 20 years after 1979, that it became a smaller, more heterogeneous group, with departmental and agency heads co-existing and working under management practices borrowed from the private sector, our study of penal policy suggests that the higher Civil Service maintained a pivotal role. Writing about the Civil Service as a whole, Page and Wright (1999) confirm this impression. They remind us that when looking at the Civil Service in this period:

> It is important to distinguish the senior positions from the bulk of the Civil Service. Change which has so far affected the majority of service-delivery areas in the Civil Service are [sic] only now reaching the top ranks. The central characteristics of an elite, permanent, impartial or objective civil service, which is selected and promoted on merit currently remain.
>
> (Page and Wright 1999, p 201)

True, by 1999 even the senior Civil Service was more heterogeneous than it once was, and there were visible tensions. However, Page and Wright maintain that the higher Civil Service had survived these changes, that the agency principle has not yet been extended "to policy functions and the senior Civil Service has not yet been contracted out" (Page and Wright 1999, p 201).

The easy formulation that the "mandarins" had become "managers" by the 1990s is therefore too facile to describe a process that combined continuity with change. (Indeed, properly rewarding the "mandarins" and encouraging the best of them to stay on as public servants is now seen as a New Labour priority. See Peter Riddle, *The Times*, 11 January 2002).

Further down the delivery chain the way in which penal services were managed was also "irrevocably" changed. To understand what was at work here we need to remind ourselves that government was putting in place mechanisms at the foot of the regulatory chain so that it could relinquish its direct role in delivering services, yet at the same time positioning itself to monitor their efficient delivery by others. As Michael Power put it, NPM represented

> a programmatic commitment to state withdrawal as direct service provider in favour of a more regulatory role through accounting, audit and other instruments. This shift has been accompanied by longer standing [New Right] ideas about the limits of government.
>
> (Power 1997, p 52)

This led to a plethora of new management practices that almost overwhelmed the Prison and Probation Services. The then Chief Inspector of Prisons acknowledged that security and financial audits, and his own operational audit, were pulling staff in too many different directions (HMSO 1997, vol. 2, para 1061). Furthermore, he went on to question the usefulness of some of the new management tools, including KPIs which had been so strongly endorsed by the Director of the Prisons Agency, though even he, it should be pointed out, had conceded under questioning that "you can walk around a prison that was doing well on performance indicators, but which actually you are not very happy about" (HMSO 1997, vol. 2, para 146; see also *The Guardian*, 20 June 2001).

General Sir John Learmont, who had been asked by the government in 1996 to look into the overall management of the Prison Service came to much the same conclusion, suggesting that far too many people now went about prisons just ticking boxes (HMSO 1997, vol. 2, para 721).

As this applied to the Probation Service, staff were asked to employ "scientific" methods of "risk assessment", which meant ticking off yet more boxes, or were pressed to conform to national standards on "breach" orders in supervising their clients. This was seen as an inappropriate attempt to introduce Taylorism into their profession where standardized responses deny the nature of the complex judgements they routinely make. Tim May put it succinctly:

> ... the achievement of accountability is clearly assisted by the nature of the task performed. A highly visible, standardized task in a predictable environment is more amenable to organizational accountability, than one which is variable and dependent for its conception and execution on the discretion of organizational officials performing differing and situationally demanding tasks. The mass production factory line is, therefore, fundamentally different from a human service organization.

(May 1995, p 55)

May's point has even more resonance in the light of the Halliday Report; *Making Punishments Work* (Home Office 2001). This envisages an even greater role for the new, nationally managed Probation Service—no quarrel with that—but the report's confidence that the new managerialism can indeed "make punishments work" has strong echoes of an earlier *positivist* tradition even though it is being promoted as part of New Labour's *modernizing* agenda for the criminal justice system as a whole.

Another way of elaborating May's critique is to suggest that while audit is inviting because its apparent transparency secures greater accountability, what often needs to be audited is not easily susceptible to measurement. For example, among the politically defined, strategic goals of government is the maintenance of a secure and safe prison system, and this might reasonably be audited around the KPIs for escapes and the number of assaults on staff and prisoners. But how do you measure, except in the most facile way, what Lord Woolf argued must be the essential strategic objective of the prison system, namely, that it must secure justice? Also, while remote, arrogant "experts" may be derided, the central irony about the audit process is that it places more power in the hands of auditors and politicians, groups which the public trusts even less than experts.

At a macro level the new institutional economics also came under fire. In the first place, doubts resurfaced about whether the quasi-markets already in place were robust enough to secure the necessary level of competition to reduce costs in the prison system. The cost/benefits of employing the private sector—always hotly disputed anyway—were said to be steadily closing by 2000 (*The Guardian*, 12 July 2001). But even more damaging, Private Finance Initiatives were discovered to have earned huge windfall dividends for private operators when reinsuring their operations at lower premiums after the initial, and most risky stage of any PFI project, was completed. The all party Parliamentary Public Accounts Committee condemned the £10.7 million which Carillon and Group 4 were said to have made from their contract to build Fazakerly prison. Another report estimated that a joint venture between US Security firm Wackenhut and the management services group Serco in which Premier Prison Services ran five prisons was said to have yielded a £7 million bounty by "bundling together" separate loans totalling £185 million (*The Observer*, 8 July 2001).

These revelations did not halt the revolution in governance we have traced. Indeed, New Labour's 2001 manifesto emphasized its determination to disaggregate government in the context of a "clear framework of national standards" and then issued the threat that, "Where the quality of public services is not improving quickly enough, alternative providers should be brought in. Where private sector providers can support public endeavour, we should use them" (Labour Party 2001, p 17). However, the fact that New Labour's conversion to NPM remains intact, that it had ramifications across the length and breadth of government, and not just in the penal services, cannot hide its obvious flaws, or that it can only deliver at maximum efficiency with the full hearted consent of those who run these services, which it demonstrably did not secure in the 1990s. If anything, practitioners, from teachers and doctors to nurses and prison officers, were hostile, agreeing with Simon Jenkins's view that NPM was a "control freak's charter" allowing government to abdicate its management responsibilities while heaping all the blame for poor services on those at the bottom of the regulatory ladder (*The Times*, 3 February 1999).

But those at the sharp end of NPM should take heart from the simple truth that it is in the nature of things that governments exercise less control than they think they do, that their attempts to control this or that service usually fail however hard sociologists try to persuade them otherwise. As Michael Power so wisely reminds us: "Efforts at social control it seems, always fail, and failure is always the condition for further attempts at control" (Power 1997, p 26).

So, the profound changes which have transformed the delivery of our penal services will not be the last; governance is never perfect. Some well-directed empirical studies into penal practice to set against some of the grander "social control" theories will demonstrate this, assuredly. As for New Labour, it has already learnt that delivery is a difficult business, that embracing the market rather than the values of public service is no panacea for securing better public services. So just how penal services will be delivered in the future remains an open question; we do not yet know, for certain, the settled trajectory of that change, and given the increasingly complex shape of the modern State apparatus, there is increasing space for both failure and resistance.

REFERENCES for *Part III*

ASI (1984) *Justice Policy* (London: ASI)

ASI (1987) *The Prison Cell* (London: ASI)

Clarke J., Cochrane A. and Maclaughlin E. (1994) *Managing Social Policy* (London: Sage)

Dunbar I. and Langdon A. (1998) *Tough Justice* (London: Blackstone)

Feinstein C. (1994) "British Economic Growth since 1948" in Floud R. and McCloskey D. (eds.) *The Economic History of Britain Since 1870*, second revised edition (Cambridge: Cambridge University Press)

Faulkner D. (Oxford, 2000). Personal communication: see the *Acknowledgements*

Faulkner D. (2001) *Crime, State and Citizen: A Field Full of Folk* (Winchester: Waterside Press)

Gamble A. (1985) *Britain in Decline* (London: Macmillan)

Habermas J. (1976) *Legitimation Crisis* (London: Heinemann)

Harding R. (1994) "Privatizing Prisons: Principle and Practice" in Biles D. and Vernon J. (eds.) *Private Sector and Community Involvement in the Criminal Justice System* (Canberra: Australian Institute of Criminology)

HMSO (1979) *May Report* (Cmnd. 7673)

HMSO (1993) *HM Prison Service Framework Document*

Home Office (1997) *Home Affairs Committee Second Report: The Management of the Prison Service (Public and Private)*, vol. 1 and vol. 2 (London: HMSO)

Home Office (2001) *Making Punishments Work: Report of a Review of the Sentencing Framework for England and Wales* (London: HMSO)

Ignatieff M. (1978) *A Just Measure of Pain: the Penitentiary in the Industrial Revolution* (London: Macmillan)

James A. L., Bottomley A. K., Clare E. and Liebling A. (1997) *Privatizing Prisons: Rhetoric and Reality* (London: Sage)

Kaye C. (1998) "Chance and Control: Politics and Management in Secure Services" *Criminal Behaviour and Mental Health*, 8, pp. 287, 295

Kellner P. and Crowther Hunt J. (1980) *The Civil Servants* (London: Raven Books)

King R. and McDermott K. (1995) *The State of Our Prisons* (Oxford: Clarendon)

Luhman N. (1982) *The Differentiation Society* (New York: Columbia University Press)

Lewis D. (1997) *Hidden Agendas* (London: Hamish Hamilton)

MacInnes J. (1987) *Thatcherism at Work* (Milton Keynes: Open University Press)

Maor M. (1999) "The Paradox of Managerialism" *Public Administration Review* Jan/Feb, vol. 15, no. 1

May T. (1995) *Probation, Politics, Policy and Practice* (Milton Keynes: Open University Press)

O'Connor J. (1973) *The Fiscal Crisis of the State* (New York: St Martin's Press)

Power M. (1997) *The Audit Society: Rituals of Verification* (Oxford: Oxford University Press)

Prison Reform Trust (1997) *Prison Privatization Report International* (London: PRT)

Prison Reform Trust (2000) *Prison Report* No. 51

Rhodes R. A. W. (1997) *Understanding Governance* (Milton Keynes: Open University Press)

Rose N. (1996) "Governing 'Advanced' Liberal Democracies" in Burney A., Osborne T. and Rose N. (eds.) *Foucault and Political Reason* (London: ULC Press)

Rose R (1977) 'Governing and Ungovernability: A Sceptical Inquiry' (Glasgow: University of Strathclyde Occasional Paper)

Rothbard M.N. (1978) *For A New Liberty: The Libertarian Manifesto* (New York: Collier/Macmillan)

Rutherford A. (1996) *Transforming Criminal Policy* (Winchester: Waterside Press)

Ryan M. (1983) *The Politics of Penal Reform* (London: Longman)

Ryan M. (1993) "Evaluating and Responding to Private Prisons in the United Kingdom" *International Journal of the Sociology of Law* 1993, vol. 21, 319–333

Ryan M. and Ward T. (1989) "Privatization and Penal Politics" in Matthews R. (ed.) *Privatizing Criminal Justice* (London: Sage)

Ryan M. and Sim J. (1999) "Power, Punishment and Prisons in England and Wales" in Weiss R. and South N. (eds.) *Comparing Prisons* (Amsterdam: Gordon and Breach)

Ryan M. and Ward T. (1989a) *Privatization and the Penal System: the American Experience and the Debate in Britain* (Milton Keynes: Open University Press)

Statham R. and Whitehead P. (1992) *Managing the Probation Service: Issues for the 90s* (London: Longman)

Windlesham Lord (1993) *Responses to Crime* (Oxford: Oxford University Press)

PART IV

Populists and Publics

In this last essay I want to engage in a discussion about the role of public opinion in the penal policy making process.

This is no simple business, not least because embedded in what we sometimes loosely refer to as "public opinion" are a number of sectional opinions organized as pressure groups whose members actively seek to influence government. Those who belong to groups like the Magistrates' Association or the National Association of Probation Officers (NAPO) are often directly involved in the allocation or delivery of punishment, while other well known pressure groups like the Prison Reform Trust are not involved in the penal system in this way, except possibly at the margins, and are therefore open to a wider, public membership. Because they are not delivering statutory services these groups sometimes, though not always, express their views more freely.

Both types of group are of special interest to those who make penal policy. Even in the days of top down, unitary government, those at the centre knew that the effective management of penal services required the active consent of those who were entrusted with the day-to-day allocation or delivery of punishment. At the same time securing the support of the well informed Howard League made selling government policies beyond the cognoscenti, to Parliament and the broader public, that much easier. Obviously such groups are not always united, and in reaching some sort of accommodation between themselves and with government, compromises have to be made, and as we have already observed, there are often some disgruntled losers.

However, keeping these groups onside as far as possible was, and continues to be, important to government. To take an example we touched on in Part II, it was to these (and allied) groups that David Faulkner's tireless efforts were directed in the long run up to the Criminal Justice Act 1991. The many speeches he made at this time were delivered to groups like Justice and the Howard League and conferences attended by NAPO delegates. He was not directly engaging with the proverbial man or woman on the Clapham omnibus.

It has always been the case, of course, as we saw in Part I over the issues of corporal and capital punishment in the 1950s and 1960s, that the broader public voice intercedes, that it gatecrashes the penal policy making elite. However, in the immediate postwar decades it was mostly an unwelcome guest, often mobilized by disgruntled groups within the policy making elite, and was an intruder that had to be managed rather than accommodated. In the postwar period it was not until the 1970s and 1980s that front bench politicians actively sought to go over the heads of the various pressure groups actively to mobilize broader public opinion in penal matters, to become overtly populist.

What lies behind this new populist thrust? How can we explain it? What, or whose, interests might it serve? What has been its impact? Is it perhaps a good thing for democracy?

These questions are easier to ask than to answer. Politicians and governments are not always clear, let alone open, about their purposes. Nor is there any agreement about whether populism fundamentally changed the processes by which penal policy is made, or even whether, and at what points, it changed the direction of penal policy per se. In other words, some see populism as a mere rhetorical backcloth that for a number of years had little impact on either process or the direction of penal policy, that the liberal elite adapted and held on almost to the new millennium.

There is the possibility too, that populism is not that easy to pigeonhole. Maybe it is more promiscuous than we imagine, capable of servicing, at different times and in different forms, a variety of masters in a variety of different ways. It is as a backdrop to this possibility that I want to use the first part of this essay, to look at the emergence of what was labelled authoritarian populism in the 1970s and work my way forward to New Labour.

AUTHORITARIAN POPULISM

The political context

I pointed out in my third essay that Britain ran into serious economic difficulties in the early 1970s. While these difficulties were understood differently, with Conservatives taking one view and Socialists another, there was a general agreement that there *was* a crisis that needed to managed. Some profound reorganization of social and economic structures was to be required if the historic agreement between capital and labour that had underpinned the postwar political consensus was to be re-negotiated or replaced.

It was by no means clear at the time, of course, that this re-structuring would be undertaken on the New Right's terms, that the market would eventually rule, to use a shorthand. Indeed, what struck many people at this time, as the lights went out during miners' strikes in 1973/4, was not so much capital's resilience, but its frailty. This partly explains why some captains of industry were prepared to embrace the high point of postwar corporatism, Labour's social contract, which was introduced by the Wilson government in 1975.

Nor was it evident, even after the fall of the first New Right inclined Conservative government in 1974, that the restructuring would take so long, or that it would involve the disruption that it did, with the return of mass unemployment, widespread and bitterly fought industrial disputes across the country and serious urban unrest, fuelled by claims of racism in places like Brixton and Liverpool. To be sure, it is too simplistic to reduce all the tensions of the 1970s and early 1980s to economic causes. For example, to interpret the resurgence of the Irish Republican movement, with all its desperate consequences, purely as a function of the economic downturn in Britain would be seriously to misrepresent the complexities that have helped to shape Ireland's troubled history.

However, manifest tensions there were, and these have been well summarized by Paul Anderson and Nyra Mann who wrote:

> Britain in 1974 was in a state of panic; IRA terrorism, militant trade unionism, the influx of immigrants, the widely publicized antics of the revolutionary Left, the country wide expansion of youth culture, the seemingly inexorable rise of vandalism, hooliganism and violent crime—all had combined to persuade substantial sections of the middle class and the political establishment that the very foundations of the British way of life were under threat. A vocal part of the right-wing intelligentsia talked of the crisis of ungovernability, former generals set up private armies; rogue elements of the security services, believing that Soviet subversion was at the root of it all, spread black propaganda about Harold Wilson and his colleagues.

(Anderson and Mann 1997)

It was against this background that an old Labour government rushed through the Prevention of Terrorism Act 1974 and Mrs Thatcher manoeuvred to secure the leadership of the Conservative Party in 1975.

Almost at once Mrs Thatcher and her new frontbench team focussed on law and order. Militant trade union activity was purposefully elided with street crime. It was argued that both showed a disrespect for the law and the authority of Parliament. The suggestion was made that Britain was drifting into industrial and political anarchy, and that the Labour government was doing nothing to prevent it. Indeed, the presence of ministers on picket lines during the Grunwick industrial dispute of 1976–8 was expressly used to suggest that Labour was even *encouraging* lawlessness (Rogaly 1977). This was reinforced by skilful advertising, and while the broadcasting authorities refused to release news footage of Grunwick to the Conservatives, Saatchi and Saatchi nevertheless ran a startling and effective billboard campaign in the summer of 1978 which asked, "Is it safe to trust another Labour government? "

This campaign was bitterly attacked by Labour in Parliament after the summer recess (see below), but it did not deflect the Conservatives whose manifesto a year later carried a special section on "The Rule of Law", immediately followed by one on "The Fight Against Crime". This first depicted Labour as having undermined the authority of Parliament; the Conservatives offered to restore this, and *within the same sentence*, to give "the right priority to the fight against crime". Tougher sentences were called for, violent criminals and the young were special targets, and there was even a promise to re-open the debate on capital punishment (Conservative Party 1979). In the subsequent election campaign 87 per cent of Conservative candidates declared themselves in support of tougher measures on law and order, they were offered as a means of securing social discipline and shoring up a crumbling political order.

This was a populist agenda, and unashamedly so. Lord Windlesham who was close to the Conservative Party at this time has written: "The Conservative campaign of 1979, the first of three under Mrs Thatcher's leadership, made more of law and order, and in a more strident and populist way, than hitherto" (Windlesham 1993, p 144).

This populist approach was vigorously challenged by the *cognoscenti*. Its members worried that such rhetoric could all too easily become counter productive. For example, what might the public demand next if tougher sentences failed to reduce crime, as they mostly had in the past? Mrs Thatcher's response was simply to reply that she was just reflecting the wishes of "the people of Britain" in these matters (Conservative Party Conference address 1977). Put in another way, she represented public opinion in its broadest and most representative sense, and she was not for turning.

So, it was "the people of Britain" the Conservatives were listening to, not to liberal pressure groups like the Howard League, not to sheltered Oxbridge educated civil servants, not to the far-from-convincing university experts on criminal behaviour, and still less to those radical criminologists whose "alternative realities" derived from the counter culture, that handmaiden of the "permissive society", that had so offended middle England by mocking order and ignoring individual responsibility for wrongdoing and the moral utility of punishment.

In its essentials, though never quite in its classic form as British society was still too deferential to entertain pure populism, Conservative rhetoric on crime and punishment in the 1970s displayed most of the basic characteristics of populism everywhere. There was a distrust of metropolitan elites, of the academy, of "backstage" policy making which favoured complicated trade-offs instead of simple, uncomplicated solutions—life sentences should mean life—

and a strong charismatic leader to convey these essential truths directly to the people (Canovan 1998). Rather as Le Penn was to encourage ordinary French men and women to ignore Parisian metropolitan elites and speak from their hearts, so Mrs Thatcher invited "the people of Britain" to have their say on law and order, to "speak out" honestly about how crime should be tackled and offenders punished. This had immense popular appeal. In the run up to the 1979 General Election law and order was the one major issue on which the Conservative Party was far ahead of Labour.

And what was wrong with this? By reflecting public opinion in its broader sense on such matters political parties are surely doing democracy a favour, so to speak? How could Mrs Thatcher and her supporters be faulted for this?

In order to respond critically to such questions I want make a short detour to re-work an instructive study undertaken by Stuart Hall and his colleagues, *Policing the Crisis* (1978). This was an inquiry into the mugging panic that swept through Britain in the 1970s during the rise of Thatcherism. It not only serves an ideological index of those "Law and Order" times, it will also help us to understand better how public opinion, which Mrs Thatcher claimed to be innocently "reflecting", in its broadest sense, is constructed.

Muggers

In the summer of 1972 a man was found stabbed to death in south London. His death was explained to the press as a "mugging gone wrong". This was then reported in the media as a frightening new strain of crime imported from America. In the months that followed a number of other muggings were reported, so it appeared that Britain was in the grip of a wave of violent crime and very tough, exemplary sentences were then handed down, not least on two or three youths who had badly beaten a defenceless man in Handsworth, Birmingham one evening in March 1993.

The panic that came to surround mugging had spread quickly. By November 1972, for example, a public opinion poll showed that one person in six felt themselves likely to be at risk from muggers. The same survey also found that 70 per cent of those interviewed wanted the government to act with a sense of urgency to tackle mugging and for 90 per cent of those interviewed this meant tougher penalties. (Just the sort of tariff increase for violent crimes that Mrs Thatcher was later to recommend in the Conservative Manifesto.) It would seem reasonable to assume that the harsh sentences which were handed out in the Handsworth case were a direct consequence of the growing public and judicial concern over a new and serious strain of crime that had first appeared in Britain just six months earlier.

What at first interested Stuart Hall and his colleagues was the speed and intensity of this reaction. They rightly point out that there was nothing new about muggings. As a street crime usually designated as robbery with assault it was, regrettably, an endemic feature of modern, urban living. So, why the great panic in August 1972 and thereafter? Had there been, they speculated, a huge increase in *overall* crime rates that had already generated a widespread feeling of unease which then triggered the crackdown on mugging *per se*? The official figures were interrogated, and even when allowances were made for their shortcomings, it appeared that there was no alarming increase in the overall crime rate in the years immediately preceding 1972. So the panic that surrounded mugging could not be attributed to any "objectively" defined crime wave. But what about those robberies with assault most closely allied to muggings, was there a significant and worrying rise here? Apparently not:

> Whatever statistics are used, whether the overall "crimes of violence" figures, or more specifically those referring to "robberies" or "muggings", it is *not* possible to demonstrate that the situation was dramatically worse in 1972 than in the period 1955–1965. In other words, it is impossible to "explain" the severity of the reaction to mugging by using evidence based on the objective, quantifiable, statistical facts.

(Hall et al. 1978, p 11)

So how was this situation, where the public reaction to a set of events clearly far outweighs their actual threat, explained? In *Policing the Crisis* (1978) the argument is that there existed a wider referential context, that the public had already come to understand mugging not only as a street crime, but as something symbolizing American urban decay, conjuring up scenes of racial conflict, dope addicts on the streets and routine police shoot outs. The idea that mugging had now reached Britain touched off this whole referential context, giving rise to widespread public anxiety. The widespread belief that what happens in America will soon happen here fuelled this *moral panic*.

The *Birmingham Post* thus justified the tough sentences handed out to the Handsworth muggers because Britain was thought to be edging towards the American experience and the public needed protection. The media has, of course, a key role to play in this signification process, passing on judges' comments that society was under threat. Judges are seen to be dispassionate upholders of law and order, so their views are respected and reported, in this case helping to reinforce the intensity of the panic. Less trusted perhaps, politicians offered their instant opinions.

The police are also party to this process, making clear their views about the need to crack down on violent criminals, and there were several well publicized police warnings at the time which suggested that things were getting out of hand in some of our cities. The police also helped to intensify the mugging panic in other ways; the argument is that they decide to target robbery with assault in parts of south-east London in the early part of 1972, setting up special patrols which led to more people coming before the courts for these offences. In other words, the police had been mobilized to combat muggings before the panic had even begun.

What this study of the mugging panic suggests is that the various agencies, *including political parties I would stress*, involved in managing, reporting and processing crime are not

> passive reactors to immediate simple and clear cut crime situations. These agencies must be understood as actively and contiguously part of the whole process to which, also, they are "reacting". They are active in defining situations, in selecting targets, in initiating "campaigns", in structuring these campaigns, in selectively signifying their actions to the public at large … They do not simply respond to "moral panics". They form part of the cycle out of which more moral panics develop.

(Hall et al. 1978, p 52)

The significance of all this for our wider argument about public opinion, and how political parties stand in relation to it, is surely clear.

Most of us are, fortunately, not routinely the victims of crime, especially violent crime. And so a lot of what we know about crime comes from the media, which, as the mugging panic demonstrates, can misrepresent the scale of the problem. Or underrepresent the problem for that matter. At the time of the mugging panic, for example, there was not much serious media debate about domestic violence against women, a point later made by those who argued that moral panic theorists on the Left, myself included, had only been telling half of the story in the 1970s, ignoring a whole range of violent crimes against women, though this charge is highly debateable (Kinsey R *et al.* 1986; Scraton (ed.) 1987).

But whichever way it is looked at, what we normally refer to as "public opinion" about crime, its extent, and what might be done about it, opinion which politicians increasingly claim to be *responding* to as good democrats, is a problematic social construct which needs to be interrogated and not merely measured and then echoed.

So why did the Conservative Party "respond" in such an unashamedly populist way in the mid-1970s, or perhaps more accurately, itself *actively become part of the cycle that both manufactured and helped to sustain its hard-line approach?*

Political opportunism
One answer would be that the Conservative Party was simply being opportunistic, and this is a reasonable place to start. Social theorists like Dario Melossi, for example, have always been aware that penal strategies are often about far more than detecting crime and punishing (or reforming) those who perpetrate it. To believe otherwise, he thinks, is to be naïve (Melossi 1994). Garland too has more recently reminded us that:

> These law and order policies frequently involve a knowing and cynical manipulation of the symbols of state power and of the emotions of fear and security which give their symbols their potency. Such politics become particularly salient where a more general insecurity—deriving from tenuous employment and fragile social relations— is widely experienced and where the State is deemed to have failed in its efforts to deliver economic security to key social groups.
>
> (Garland 1996)

The possibility that something like this was happening in the 1970s is compelling. Senior Conservatives must have understood that fuelling public anxieties about law and order, demanding tougher sentences for offenders, would resonate in a society at a time when the postwar social democratic consensus was faltering and the economy winding down. Its populism was an instrument for mobilizing a wider *authoritarian consensus* to legitimize a crackdown on "irresponsible" trade unionists, the "overblown" Welfare State and the "permissive society" that was necessary to secure the new market economy. It was not about tackling crime *per se*, except possibly indirectly.

Marxists would take the argument one step further by suggesting that the Conservative Party's programme was initiated in the interests of a British *ruling class* (or *class fraction*). This had imposed its own ends on society as a whole by securing the postwar accommodation between capital and labour, largely if not entirely, on its own terms. However, in the economic turbulence of the 1970s the *hegemony* secured by largely peaceful means after 1945 was no longer sustainable and the interests of capital had to be secured by mobilizing a new, *authoritarian consensus*. Ratcheting up the rhetoric on law and order was all a part of this wider process, of mobilizing the "silent majority" for the struggle ahead.

This Marxist view had only minority support at the time. However, the less doctrinaire view that penal populism was orchestrated by the Conservative Party in the 1970s, *in part at least,* as a mechanism to help manage the stresses imposed by painful economic, social and political adjustments, still seems as convincing to me now as it did then, and this is a view shared by many other non-Marxists.

The Conservative riposte

Conservative apologists, inevitably, interpret the 1970s somewhat differently, indeed they simply echo Margaret Thatcher. Lord Windlesham, for example, while coyly admitting to an element of electoral opportunism by suggesting that once the "hubbub" of the 1979 General Election was over Conservative policy makers took more serious soundings, goes on to suggest that these:

> Quieter and more reflective voices began to move in the same direction as the "loud angry crowd. Very angry and very loud", whose constant chant was that the only way to control crime was by strengthening the police, improving rates of detection, and punishing prisoners more severely.
>
> (Windlesham 1993, p 145)

Lord Windlesham is not entirely clear whose these quieter voices were, though he admits that the government from 1979 onward was "less inclined" to the habit of taking "disinterested advice" from bodies like the Advisory Council on the Penal System.

But more significant for our purposes, there is no suggestion here that the Conservative Party was in any sense involved in *constructing* the "large angry crowd": that its leaders interacted with at best, or at worst, manipulated the public by selecting symbols which played on its worst fears about crime and punishment. No, Conservative politicians simply *responded* to public opinion. Nor is there any appreciation of the subsequent irony, that is, of moderate Conservative home secretaries being heckled at Party conferences, no sense that the Conservative leadership had uncorked the populist bottle for their own, wider political purposes only to be consumed by its simplicities when trying to devise a workable, long term penal strategy once they were returned to government.

Quite the opposite, in fact. Lord Windlesham and his senior political colleagues such as William Whitelaw, and later, Douglas Hurd, are portrayed as enlightened pragmatists, who continued to be willing to work with David Faulkner's liberal *ensemble* to achieve a more rational course for criminal justice as a whole. This, as my previous essays have indicated, is not *entirely* disingenuous. The problem is that their *coup d'état* in the form of the Criminal Justice Act 1991 was rapidly overturned. A number of sensational tabloid attacks on the working of the Act, plus the opposition of some members of the legal profession, and New Labour's hard-line conversion were enough to sink it. There had been enough support among the liberal *cognoscenti* to guarantee the original Bill's passage through Parliament, but that support did not run deep.

This reversal should not surprise us. In the 1980s other senior Conservative politicians were happy to concede that in penal matters the popular press counted for more than informed opinion:

> The "standard lobbies" are not very important to Conservative governments. Not only are they completely out of line with public opinion, but no Conservative home secretary is going to go to bed quaking and shivering because one of those groups is austerely critical of him. The most effective lobbying is actually in the newspapers.

> (Quoted by Rock 1990, p 227)

And among the most influential press lobbyists was Rupert Murdoch whose "red tops" were quick to pounce on any "pissing liberals" among Mrs Thatcher's *entourage* (Sim 2000).[1]

The tension that this populism generated at the heart of the policy making process into the 1980s is well illustrated by looking at the Conservative government's response to the treatment of victims in the criminal justice system.

Victims

Rank and file Conservatives were very much in favour of helping victims in the 1980s. As far as most Conservatives were concerned far too much attention had been given to, and time and money wasted on, criminals. The needs of victims on the other hand, had mostly been forgotten.

The victims' movement, as we saw in my second essay, was like most social movements, a complicated one, combining different and sometimes conflicting strands. One of these strands was Joan Jonker's Victims of Violence group founded in Liverpool in 1977. Jonker was a skilful populist who both caught, and contributed towards, the awakening of the public interest in victims by courting popular tabloid editors such as Geoffrey Levey of *The Daily Express*, and broadcasters like Desmond Lapsley who, with her help, produced a television documentary about elderly victims, *The Old Can't Run Fast Enough*. In this role Jonker helped in the social construction of the victim as the frail, white-haired old lady terrorized by the young mugger. Evidence that the old were mostly not victims of such crime was an inconvenient piece of informed opinion the tabloids chose to overlook.

The flavour of Jonker's powerful rhetoric, which she often displayed in the company of the young William Hague, with its simple, direct appeal to conviction politics, is captured in these comments about offenders whose plight she blames on professional "do gooders":

> They are the people who have fought vigorously against any sort of realistic punishment for offenders. It is they who have made excuses for the criminal so there is no longer any shame attached to crime. They have allowed the young, the weak

---

[1] Should this example seem to be unfairly singling out the Murdoch press, I would draw readers' attention to Julie Burchill's article in *The Guardian* where the epithet "crook suckers" instead of "pissing" is applied to those liberals who, she argues, identify with criminals while ignoring the plight of their victims (*Guardian Weekend*, 2 March 2002).

willed and violent members of our society to believe that they can get away with anything. They have ruined the youth of our society. Instead of strength they have shown weakness, even to the most violent thugs who know that if they are caught they can rely on someone, be it a probation officer, social worker or solicitor to make excuses for them. It is they who are the real culprits.

(Jonker 1986, pp 219/220)

One of Jonker's techniques was to concentrate on individual victims and their plight, a technique that was also adopted by the *Kilroy* television show in the 1980s which used personal testimony: "*Kilroy* actively sought out victims who were willing to tell their own stories in a public forum that centred on atomizing problems of human interest" (Rock 1998, p 237). Not even campaigning pressure groups were encouraged to participate, still less academics who might try to interpret their experience with some wider body of knowledge that could be useful to those who made policy. No experts were allowed, no structured debate about the rights of others in the criminal justice system. About this populist technique Bernard Crick has recently observed:

Increasingly ... presenters will ask a relative of a victim what the punishment should be, or draw from an allegedly "ordinary person" a snap, prejudiced and often ignorant opinion. Well, if they are not representative, at least they are an "authentic voice"—that magic word that links populism high and low.

(*The Guardian*, 19 August 2000)

Jonker's rhetoric, and Kilroy's practice, worried senior, liberal civil servants in the Home Office. Mike Hough, joint author of the British Crime Survey, raised the issue uppermost in their minds in 1984 when he questioned this new, strident interest in the plight of victims by asking, "Is it populism or is it democracy?" (Rock 1990, p 331). So those making criminal justice policy in the Home Office spent much of the 1980s trying to sidestep the likes of Jonker and Kilroy by encouraging the altogether less strident National Association of Victims' Support Schemes (NAVSS). This Association at least acknowledged that tackling crime and punishment was a complicated business which would not be served by those using the press to turn personal testimony into vigilantism.

Steering this course was far more difficult in the populist climate that the Conservative Party had helped to create. Populist appeals had delivered the votes all right, several times over by now, in fact. The problem was that these appeals had made pursuing a more considered and sustainable penal policy that much more difficult.

Thus, despite the Conservatives' encouragement of the NAVSS, and its success in reducing the number of imprisoned young offenders (Newburn 1995) against the tide of its own rhetoric of "the short, sharp shock", the Conservative Party's overall record paints a different picture. For example, Mrs Thatcher's first administration put in place the biggest prison building programme since Victorian times, significantly increased the already long prison sentences for more serious offences and, with the strong support of Leon Brittan, minister of State at the Home Office, placed restrictions on those entitled to parole. In 1990 prisons across the country erupted in protest over their conditions, and HMP

Strangeways was rendered almost unusable in the worst prison riot of the twentieth century. In 1978, the year before the Conservatives were re-elected to government, the average daily prison population (men and women) stood at over 45,000. A year after it left office, in 1998, the combined population stood at over 65,000, and was rising.

Enlightened pragmatists like Whitelaw, Hurd and Windlesham are partly responsible for this long punitive drift. It did not all begin with the avowedly populist Home Secretary Michael Howard in the mid-1990s. Making Howard the scapegoat is far too convenient. Perhaps these Tory grandees took the view that the price of securing the market in the 1980s was worth this social damage. Politicians make such messy, cost/benefit calculations, albeit sometimes unconsciously, that is the nature of their business, and the victory of neo-liberalism was a huge prize. It would be naïve for penal lobbyists, or academic criminologists for that matter, to think otherwise.

More generously, it might be argued that Whitelaw, Hurd and Windlesham did their best in the 1980s. The problem was that the Conservative Party is a broad church whose populist sentiments on penal questions, once uncorked by others, were quite beyond their control. Either way, they are more culpable than most, and more culpable than they publicly admit.

I will return later to consider whether the populism that helped to fuel these policies can be wholly laid at the Conservatives' door, to consider whether or not there were (and are) other forces at work changing the nature of modern democracies. I will also explore the allied, and not insignificant possibility, that in a responsive democracy a tension between populist and informed opinion is no bad thing.

But first, what of Labour in the 1970s and 1980s? If the Conservatives were, as they saw it anyway, listening to the broader public, who were Labour politicians listening to as they lurched into the political wilderness, untrusted on law and order and just about every other issue except the National Health Service?

Old Labour to New Labour

The Labour Party rarely debated law-and-order issues at its party conferences in the postwar period, and penal policy, aside from capital punishment, was discussed almost never (Ryan 1983). The Party was more at ease with traditionalist home secretaries when in office, and tolerated rather than applauded its more liberal ones, like Roy Jenkins in the 1960s. The broad cross-party consensus on these issues was reinforced by the shared belief that these complex matters were best dealt with in a non-partisan manner. There was a suspicion among the Party faithful that perhaps Labour paid too much attention to quirky liberal experts like Lord Longford, or wrongly implied a simple causal relationship between poverty and crime, but on the whole Party members left the detail of these difficult matters to their leaders.

Breaking with this consensus took Labour by surprise. Party spokespersons railed against the Conservatives over the Saatchi and Saatchi posters, deploring their simplicity, arguing that all western societies were faced with rising levels of crime, and that understanding what was happening was a matter of the utmost "seriousness", hardly the subject for a frivolous poster campaign that played on people's worst fears (*Hansard* vol. 957, col. 635). The Conservatives responded by taunting Labour, claiming that the party had previously implied that law and order had been blown up by the "wicked Tories", that Labour had been drawn into a conference debate on the issue "kicking and screaming", that only now was the Party showing a degree of realism, that at last "it was being moved by the pressure of public opinion towards the view that we [the Conservatives] have been putting forward" (*Hansard* vol. 957, col. 628).

That Labour had never sought really to engage public opinion on this issue was seen by some within the party as a tactical error. Their argument, and it needs to be stressed, that they did not subscribe to the New Right's analysis of Britain's predicament, or look to the market for solutions, at least at the time, nevertheless was that Labour had seriously misread its own public, that however much the Conservatives might have manipulated public opinion, its strategy did at least have *some* bearing on reality. For example, in *Law and Order Arguments for Socialism* (1981) the late Ian Taylor wrote:

> From the moment of achieving power within the Tory Party in 1975, this radical–right leadership has carried out a campaign against liberal and progressive politics generally, insisting that the educational, welfare and crime politics of both Labour and liberal Tory governments were the cause of the breakdown in social order. Throughout 1978, and during the election campaign of 1979, the Tory leadership … proclaimed that the victory of the new Conservative Party would result in the restoration of order in social life ... The freeing of the market from excessive interference by the State would encourage individuals to take a new responsibility … Social discipline would therefore emerge out of individual self-discipline.
>
> (Taylor 1981, pp x and xi)

He goes on, and the emphasis is Taylor's, not mine:

> The attack was effective primarily because of the *real* limitations that existed in the bureaucratic form of the British Welfare State and also because postwar social democracy *had* failed to provide a sense of social order. The anxieties experienced by working people and the elderly living in dilapidated and isolated housing developments *are* real, and these *are* areas in which there is a greater risk of vandalism and street crime generally than others. Large numbers of traditional Labour voters reported that they had changed their vote to Mrs Thatcher in 1979 on the basis of the attacks she made on Labour's record on crime.
>
> (Taylor 1981, p xiv)

So Taylor did not dispute that the Conservatives had employed populist tactics, that they had offered simple solutions to complex problems of law and order, and that this was to secure support for a wider political agenda, but this had succeeded, he argued because it touched on the realities of lived experience among many Labour voters. You cannot, as it were, construct a moral panic out of nothing. About some of the more critical, "alternative realities" on offer from the Left he observed:

> There has been a tendency in recent years for liberal criminologists, and especially for those who work entirely in universities or colleges to want to deny or qualify fears,

especially about crime waves, by pointing to the statistical facts about crime, or by stressing that many of the popular anxieties are the results of moral panics, resulting in over sensitive reactions of the media to particular events. This kind of liberal criminology has been extremely weak in recent years, as working people have increasingly come to experience real material, social and personal problems.

(Taylor 1981, p 9)

But Taylor was no simple "Realist", to use a shorthand applied to other criminologists at the time (for example, Young and Lea 1984). He was too much of a political economist steeped in traditional Labour politics to take that particular route. He argued rather, that the nature of the postwar settlement between capital and labour could never have resolved the inherent conflict between the two. The result was an under resourced Welfare State, unable to meet real social needs, in the hands of bureaucratic, middle class, professional elites who increasingly "imposed" their *Statist* solutions on an increasingly alienated working class. This imposition from above, combined with the associated failure of the corporately managed mixed economy to sustain economic growth in the 1970s, led ordinary people to experience the State, "not as a 'beneficiary' but [as] a powerful bureaucratic imposition" (Taylor 1981; Hall 1979, p 18) .

This was the fertile ground on which the New Right's populism was built. Getting the great weight of the State "off their backs" seemed like a good idea to many people, including a good number of Labour supporters who rallied to Mrs Thatcher in the hope that she would take their *real* law and order fears seriously.

Law and Order Arguments for Socialism (1981), with its practical, interim agenda around police accountability, democratizing the magistracy, strengthening the jury system, re-shaping the Prison Service with a little help from PROP, and returning adjudications of "dangerousness" to local communities, was Taylor's radical Labour agenda for re-engaging the State with its public in matters of law and order.[2] He believed his programme would coincide with the "lived realities" of ordinary people and appeal to a broader public. He was supremely confident that Thatcher's 1979 electoral victory would never be repeated, that people would come to appreciate the need for a remodelled interventionist State in modern complex societies (Taylor 1981). It is all too clear that he massively underestimated the weight of the ideological shift that was then taking place, and this partly explains why this text by one of Britain's most gifted criminologists almost sank without trace. It was out of time.

It has also been argued by other leading criminologists that Labour's failure to connect with its natural supporters was further exacerbated in the 1980s by the New Left which, having taken over Labour's moribund local parties and captured the local State, then ran it in alliance with a new series of groupings which it "borrowed" from the Frankfurt School of the 1960s and 1970s. "Having constituted these new groups it then attempted to strike much the same set of

---

[2] He was particularly anxious that local communities should be involved in assessing "dangerousness", that this should not just be left to officials and so-called experts (Taylor 1981, p 141). It is therefore likely that he would have supported, in principle at least, the government's intention to include lay persons on local panels to monitor serious sex offenders after their release (*Independent*, 22 June 2002).

relations as its predecessors had with their electoral base" (Corrigan P. *et al.* 1988, p 13). That is, they became remote, talking among themselves, creating a mutually "reinforcing circle of minority representatives, police monitoring groups, political committees and community leaders".

The paradigm example of this style of politics would have been the GLC with its Police Committee and its Women's Committee. The fact that that the former did more than any other local authority, except possibly Manchester, to raise the issue of police accountability, that it supported groups like INQUEST (which raised serious questions about black deaths in custody), or that the GLC Women's Committee at last gave a public profile to issues around sexual offences against women and children, is seen of little consequence in this account. Corrigan *et al.* argued that even if those involved in such groups had been serious about building a new form of cultural politics which went beyond the moribund class politics of Labour, they were as much a liability in electoral terms as the old guard, the machine politicians they had replaced.

However, what is particularly intriguing about this explanation of Labour's continuing "disconnection", first set out in Corrigan *et al's* Fabian pamphlet in 1988, is that while it echoes Ian Taylor's critique of unresponsive local (often Labour), bureaucracies, it does so in very different language. Instead, it begins to mimic the language of the new managerialism, claiming that welfare bureaucracies have few clearly defined Key Performance Indicators, that they themselves continue to define what the public needs rather than responding to what their "customers" want. They still see the public as "passive receivers of services rather than as active citizens who have rights over public institutions". This is the market language of the New Right, and now New Labour, where the public as consumers of criminal justice services is invited to enter into a new contract with the government, where matters of distributive justice are assumed to be settled, and where accountability is reduced to ensuring that measures are now in place to guarantee that service being efficiently delivered.

This reflects what was fast becoming a growing consensus around criminal justice. But the consensus was more than just around the effective management of services. It was about New Labour accepting and then embracing, though arguably on its own terms, the disciplinary agenda that the Conservatives had translated into public opinion so successfully as "common sense". When this happened, exactly, has assumed a mythical importance among commentators, with each identifying what was for them the defining moment.

"Tough on crime and tough on the causes of crime"

Philip Gould, an influential New Labour apologist, for example, believes that this acceptance was signalled with Tony Blair's speech following the murder of James Bulger in 1993. While attacking directly the liberal individualist consensus that had developed over crime, Blair nonetheless used the language of "right and wrong" and "punishment". It was this, argued Gould:

> Perhaps more then anything else ... [that] ... reconnected Labour to its electoral base. Most people believe in punishment, they believe in right and wrong, and they believe in discipline and order. That for so long Labour had denied this ... was unacceptable to large numbers of the electorate who had suffered the consequences of crime on a

daily basis. Now, what Blair said seems common sense; then, it seemed, in the annals of many on the Left, iconoclastic.

(Gould 1998, pp 188/189)

For Dunbar and Langdon the defining moment was Blair's willingness to admit during a weekend radio interview that, "You've got to be prepared to punish". It was this very public statement that enabled New Labour to leap free "in one bound" from the "shackles that weighed it down" since 1979 (Dunbar and Langdon 1998, p 102).

Tony Blair's biographer, Stephen Rentoul, writes an account that is not incompatible with these views. Certainly he believes that Blair's performance on law and order at the time of James Bulger's murder helped to propel him to the leadership of his party (Rentoul 1995).

It is possible to read into all of these accounts, though Gould's especially, a measure of analytical sloppiness, ignoring as they do the obvious truth that *every* Labour statement on crime in the years between 1979 and 1993 had at the very least *implied* the language of "right and wrong" and of "punishment". After all, defining in law what is considered to be right and wrong behaviour, proposing punishments for those who break the law, and then being held accountable to Parliament for those who administer these punishments is actually what politicians do, or what they present themselves to the electorate as being prepared to do. There can be no democratic politics without the implicit recognition of such language.

If we go beyond this analytical sloppiness, however, what is being suggested here is that, at this time, New Labour was *perceived* by the wider public to have accepted the "punitive populism" (Bottoms 1995; Sparks 1996) of the New Right. In "the war against crime", to borrow a phrase much loved by politicians since it first entered the modern public lexicon (HSMO 1964), New Labour had now moved its tanks onto the New Right's lawn.

This *was* a decisive shift, and it was sold to traditional Labour welfarists by the formula that the party was being "tough on crime and tough on the causes of crime" (the phrase was, in fact, Gordon Brown's) (Rentoul 1995). This was the magic hyphen that joined both right and left wings of the Party. On the one hand, crime among the young, for example, needed to involve punishment, and punishment delivered far more effectively and more swiftly than the Conservatives were delivering it, but the structural features which in some cases might have contributed towards this offending behaviour, be it poor parenting or limited job prospects, likewise needed to be addressed because, unlike Mrs Thatcher and her abrasive, liberal individualism, New Labour *did* believe that there is something called "society" that imposes both rights and obligations.

In this way, through this magic hyphen, a united New Labour embraced the popular, Conservative consensus on the need to be tough on crime and punishment. But where did the sectional, liberal publics fare in relation to this consensus under New Labour?

REPOSITIONING THE PUBLICS

The role of sectional opinions in the policy making process was the subject of a lively debate in the 1980s. Douglas Hurd, for example, in a thoughtful 1986 lecture to the Royal Institute of Public Administration—long before the rise of the New Public Management—argued that ideally Parliament and ministers should free themselves to a much greater extent from pressure groups who "interpose" themselves between the Executive and Parliament on the one hand, and between Parliament and the electorate on the other. He felt that too often policy outcomes reflected the balance of forces between these rival sectional opinions rather than reflecting the public interest. Ministers, he felt, should arrive at their own view of the public interest. Whether he felt this even more keenly when the lobby for private prisons got underway at the Home Office is an interesting question. Our evidence suggests that he probably *did*, at first keeping his distance from this lobby, just as he held himself apart from the traditional penal lobby, especially the Howard League.

Interestingly, however, Hurd did *not* argue for a greater involvement of public opinion in its broadest sense, though he would no doubt have claimed that ministers needed to understand the public mood. Nor was he suggesting sectional interests should be excluded altogether, rather he was arguing that in deciding what the public interest is on this or that issue, ministers should be less subject to the pressure of sectional opinions, sectional interests, each invariably masquerading as the public interest.

When he became Home Secretary Jack Straw echoed this opinion. He too wanted to re-position sectional opinions, but was keener than the patrician Douglas Hurd to ensure that in any dialogue on crime and punishment the public had to be listened to, that their "lived experience" had to be actively taken on board. He was not interested in simply using public opinion as a rhetorical backcloth, as the Conservatives had done in the 1970s and 1980s, and then expecting to be left to get on with the difficult (backstage) business of making penal policy. The traditional way of doing business, of leaving such sensitive matters to metropolitan elites, was simply not good enough.

During the passage of the Crime and Disorder Bill (1998) Straw wrote a seminal article for *The Times*, "Crime and Old Labour's Punishment", in which he argued:

> What pleases me most is not just the content of the Bill, but the fact that it is rooted in the experience of local communities across the country. The Bill includes the new Anti-social Behaviour Orders to help to combat the kind of neighbourhood nuisance and disorder which faced my constituents, major reforms of the youth justice system (including swifter procedures), measures to ensure young offenders and their parents face up to the consequences of their wrongdoing ...
>
> There are the new Sex Offender Orders which—alongside extended supervision for those released from prison—will give the police and other agencies extra powers to deal with those who prey on children. Under these civil orders, paedophiles could be prevented from behaving in a threatening way, such as loitering outside school gates or hanging around school playgrounds ...
>
> For too many years the concerns of those who have lived in areas undermined by crime and disorder were ignored or overlooked by people whose comfortable notions

of human behaviour were matched by their comfortable distance from its worst excesses.

And for all its claims to socialist principles and a working class base, the Labour Party in the early 1980s conspired in this approach by handing over policy to a vanguard of single-issue pressure groups.

The Labour Programme published in 1982 served as a prelude to the 1983 General Election manifesto ... It represented the zenith of pressure group pressure. Running to 280 pages it included every conceivable demand and request of just about every organization that could be bothered to make one ...

[But] there was very little of substance on law and order. There was no pressure group speaking up for the interest of those who had suffered from the shocking increase in criminal behaviour. So the victim's voice went unheard, even though it was Labour's natural constituency which was the most affected by this rise in crime. As a result our analysis and solutions were rejected by the very people we sought to help.

It was only when my party began to ensure that our policies were relevant to our constituents themselves that we started a serious examination of the problems which communities face and how we could begin to solve them. I make no apology for this.

In the period before last year's General Election, my colleagues and I spent much of our time talking to those at the sharp end of the problems of crime and disorder victims, the police, magistrates, local councils. By doing so, we were able to bring forward coherent and workable solutions that formed the basis of our manifesto last May, and enabled us to move swiftly to implement our plans.

All this has been marked out by a new approach to policy making through which Tony Blair transformed the Labour Party from a party of opposition to one of government. This is also why I believe that the Crime and Disorder Bill represents the triumph of democratic politics—in truth a victory for local communities over detached metropolitan elites. And for me, it also represents the advantages of an electoral system founded on the direct relationship between voters and their MP. Sitting in constituency surgeries every other week, speaking to people, hearing their worries, can be an uncomfortable and tiring experience. But is always enlightening. It is a reminder to politicians of whose interests we are supposed to represent.

I am not against interest groups. They play an important role in our plural democracy. Indeed, many significant reforms over the last 30 years may not have occurred without them. I have in government, as in opposition, sought to talk with interested organizations whenever I can, and I hope that most will agree that my door has been open to discuss proposals and hear suggestions for improving the criminal justice system.

But elected politicians should be very wary of the dangers of becoming the agents of sectional interest and of ignoring the concerns of those who elect them.

(The Times, 8 April 1998)

So, public opinion broadly defined, diligently gathered through constituency surgeries and augmented, no doubt, by opinion polls and the findings from focus groups, was to be Labour's primary constituency, not the special publics made up of what Straw was later to refer to as the BMW owning Hampstead liberals who had disproportionately influenced policy making over the years. Eager to demonstrate this commitment, Straw went beyond the hallowed columns of *The Times,* talking regularly to the "red tops", especially *The Daily Mirror.*

Also writing in support of the Crime and Disorder Bill (1998) Tony Blair chose the tabloid *The News of the World* to stress his commitment to govern in the interest of "ALL the country" (*The News of the World,* May 1998). This claim to be looking to the interest of "ALL the country", of responding to public opinion broadly defined, above sectional opinions, beyond Parliament and the parties even, was consistent with Blair's speech to New Labour's recently elected MPs in 1997 where he had proclaimed: "We are not the masters now. The people are the masters. We are the servants of the people. We will never forget that". (Quoted in Rawnsley 2001, p xiii).

Andrew Rawnsley has reminded us that this was a deliberate, populist inversion of Labour's jibe at the defeated Conservative benches after the 1945 General Election that Labour members were the masters now (Rawnsley 2001). This attitude, it smacked of Parliamentary arrogance even at the time, led to the gradual isolation of Labour from the people, and not just their own supporters. This could not be allowed to happen again, and especially not on an issue like law and order where Labour's natural supporters *had* lost out.

The strength of this populist commitment was reinforced a few months later in an article by Philip Gould, analysing New Labour's landside and looking to the future. He wrote:

My final modernizing assumption is that progressive governments now demand new forms of contact with the electorate. Disconnection from the electorate has been a systematic failure of Labour. In the 1950s it failed to connect to the new mood of consumer aspiration. In the 1980s the break between party and people became almost terminal. Opinion polling and focus groups play a part in winning elections and hopefully winning re-election. But that is not the real point. I am essentially a populist. I believe that the opinions of people who lack influence and access to the media matter just as much as those with louder and more public voices. Any progressive party and any progressive government should listen to the voice of the people. Opposition to focus groups and opinion polling is a continuation of the progressive elitism that had plagued Labour since its formation. Labour is a people's party and the people's voice should be heard.

(*The Guardian,* 24 August 1999)

Liberal fears

New Labour's rhetoric at this time was very unsettling for penal lobby groups. To be sure, sectional opinions were not to be discarded, but they had been given notice that their hitherto privileged position could no longer be taken for granted: broader public opinion was going to be regularly canvassed and taken into account. So New Labour had not only embraced the mantra of punitive populism, that was worrying enough, but it had also embraced a way of doing business the lobby believed was likely to reinforce it.

Concern over Labour's dialogue with the "red tops" stretched beyond the penal lobby. For example, Roy Hattersley, unashamedly representing traditional Labour, warned about the dangers of "dumbing down", of seeking "simple solutions", only to be accused by Jack Straw of being "snobbish" (Ryan 1999).

A similar, divided response accompanied the events surrounding a series of violent attacks on suspected paedophiles in the summer of 2000. These began on the Paulsgrove council estate in Portsmouth. They led to suspected paedophiles and their families, some of them quite innocent, having to flee their homes rather than face protracted and violent demonstrations outside (and damage to) their properties. These demonstrations were orchestrated by a number of mothers pushing their children in wheelchairs with placards carrying messages such as, "Kill the paedophiles", "Don't house them, hang them"(*The Guardian*, 10 August 2000). Children wore T-shirts inscribed with slogans such as, "Keep the Perverts from our Kids" (*The Times*, 10 August 2000). Some of the children were clearly too young to walk. When an organization called Antimatter leafleted hundreds of homes in south London naming suspected paedophiles at least two people were wrongly identified and the police were forced to call neighbours to explain the mistake (*The News Shopper*, Lewisham and Catford, 9 August 2000). In Manchester a man was attacked for resembling a suspected paedophile (*The Guardian*, 4 August 2000) and even more absurdly, a *paediatrician* had her house attacked and was forced to leave the neighbourhood!

This outburst of vigilantism was prompted by the decision of the red top *News of the World* to publish the names and pictures of convicted paedophiles. It was done in order to gain support for the newspaper's Sarah's Law Campaign. This had been sparked off by the tragic abduction and murder by a paedophile of young Sarah Payne in Sussex. The campaign wanted, among other things, the right of parents to know the whereabouts of child sex offenders living in their neighbourhood, and that life sentences handed out to paedophiles should mean life. The campaign also called for: an extension of sex offender orders to include certain "high risk" paedophiles who at that time fell outside of the sex offender registration requirements; for the right of victims to know why this or that sentence had been passed; and to be informed of the release date of those who had abused them. (Sarah's law was consciously modelled on Megan's law that had been introduced in the USA a few years earlier.) *The News of the World* claimed to have collected 400,000 signatures in favour of its proposals. Polls carried out by Sky Television and Carlton TV also indicated widespread support for such a measure (*The News of the World*, 6 August 2000).

The response to this moral panic was instructive. To begin with there was widespread condemnation of the violence involved. Even *The News of the World* argued that such lawlessness was wrong and likely to be counter productive. There was, however, less agreement over whether or not the editor of *The News of the World*, Rebekah Wade, should have published the photographs which had prompted this lawlessness. Some senior journalists, Charles Moore (*The Daily Telegraph*) and Peter Kellner (*The Guardian*), were strongly critical; they were in turn attacked by *The News of the World* for living in "comfortable surroundings" which were so far divorced from the "real world" of Paulsgrove that their opinions hardly mattered. This rebuke was echoed in the letters from readers who berated the entrenched "we know better mob", "the do-gooders" and the "great and the good" (*The News of the World*, 6 August 2000). The Conservative frontbench spokesperson Ann Widdecombe who had disowned what she saw as a "lynch mob mentality" was also attacked, as was Michael Howard who was worried about—of all things—the safety of these "perverts" (*The News of the World* , 6 August 2000).

New Labour minister Chris Smith on the other hand was reported to have agreed that, "It is a noble motive to want to ensure the issue of paedophiles is more widely understood and children properly protected". Home Office minister Paul Boateng also agreed that: "There were important arguments to be had" (*The News of the World*, 6 August 2000). This was echoed in a *Guardian* leader (11 August 2000). This pointed out that while not all paedophile activity represents a homicidal threat to children, and that such activity occurs in all social classes, the leader nonetheless acknowledged that the protesters enjoyed a lot of sympathy around the country, that if Paulsgrove had indeed become the dumping ground for paedophiles then the residents had "every right to be furious", and that the liberal arguments of "civilized society" conducted in Parliamentary tea rooms and among Bishops were likely to cut no ice on estates like Paulsgrove. This line of argument was given further licence in an article which appeared sometime later in *The Guardian* where Jonathan Freedland reflected that:

> Last summer presented a clear display of this brand of liberal snobbism, when the citizens of the Paulsgrave estate mobilized in admittingly ugly protest against paedophiles living there were drowned in metropolitan derision—a wave of broadsheet hysteria. Their accusers were *cognoscenti* who could adopt an impeccably liberal stance towards released child molesters safe in the knowledge that none of them would be housed next door to them.
>
> (*The Guardian*, 1 August 2001)

On the basis of his article in *The Times*, Jack Straw would almost certainly have relished this attack on the arrogance of the metropolitan elite, and presumably would not have bridled too much when a reader wrote to *The News of the World* complaining that it was all right for the government to put paedophiles back into the community, but "They're hardly going to live next door to Jack Straw are they?" (*The News of the World*, 6 August 20001). (How the *cognoscenti* deal with their own paedophiles is not something that receives much attention. If they are not shipped off to live next door to Jack Straw just where do they go?) It is difficult to believe that he had not been the subject of this sort of attack during one of his sometimes "uncomfortable" surgeries, or that parental concerns over the safety of their children had not cropped up in one of Philip Gould's focus groups. Indeed, in signalling, in *The Times* and in Parliament, the need to keep track of paedophiles Straw had publicly *joined the cycle that helped construct the moral panic* around paedophiles, just as Conservative politicians had contributed to the construction of the mugging panic in the 1970s.

But what do we make of the Paulsgove disturbances in the context of our argument? The first and most obvious point is that it re-kindled old liberal fears about public opinion; that is to say, if policy makers ask the public to judge on penal questions then they are likely to respond in an ignorant, illiberal way. Looked at in this way, it could be argued that Jack Straw and New Labour got what they deserved. Like the Conservatives before them, albeit for different reasons perhaps—by this I mean they were hardly in the middle of a struggle between capital and labour to secure the market as in the 1970s and 1980s—New Labour uncorked the populist bottle for their own political purposes and now had to live with the consequences. One can almost hear old Labour's Roy Hattersley and his liberal Hampstead friends saying, "I told you so". (Penal lobbyists from the 1940s and 1950s would barely have recognized the policy processes at work here.)

I will return to consider the implications of this important argument later. In the meantime, I want to investigate what I here loosely refer to as academic fears, to see how some academic players have interpreted this apparent intrusion of the public into matters of penal policy.

Academic fears

I want to take as my starting point Professor Andrew Rutherford's well reviewed text, *Transforming Criminal Policy* (Rutherford 1996), where he discusses, among others, the work of Scandinavian criminologists Nils Christie and Thomas Mathiesen. I should make it clear that I have great respect for the opinions of all these academics, and that my opinions on many penal issues are not a good deal different from theirs. But even more important, all have been actively involved, as I have, in the penal lobby, in trying to influence the direction of penal policy. So I am particularly interested in what they have to say about penal policy making and the role of public opinion.

Rutherford is much impressed by Nils Christie's idea of a moral community that depends on "the involvement of an inner core of decision makers, consisting of experts and other elites". Rutherford takes the existence of such a community as being necessary to sustain a liberal penal policy. He gives the example of Finland where no more than 25 key decision makers, civil servants, judges and administrators were involved in reducing that country's unusually large prison population. Members of this group often met informally, sometimes in each others homes. He specifically identifies David Faulkner as being a leading light in sustaining such a moral community in Britain (Rutherford 1996). He is far too modest to say this, but as a one-time chairperson of the Howard League, Rutherford also contributed to the informal gatherings that constituted this moral community here in Britain.

Building on the idea of a moral community, and adapting a framework used by Thomas Mathiesen, Rutherford tries to set his own schematic framework to position some of the various publics I have identified. So there is an *outer* sphere of opinion that involves what I have identified as the broader public, including the mass media. Then there is an *inner* sphere. These are the people who run the criminal justice system, including prison administrators, magistrates and the like. Finally there is the *kernel*, or the moral community. There is, of course, a degree of overlap between these three groups. For example, there are many progressive criminal lawyers, justices' clerks and probation officers who claim a place in the *kernel*. Also, of course, the relationship between these groups is always in a state of flux. The moral community will often have its back to the wall, trying to sustain a principled liberal position against the latest public outrage. So for example, the moral community in Britain managed to secure the Criminal Justice Act 1991, but could not sustain it, the *inner* and *outer* spheres intruded and upset the proposed new order. Similarly, the moral community in The Netherlands lost ground in the early 1990s (van Swaaningen and de Jonge 1995).

Setbacks like this are normal; the moral community will need to re-group, devise new strategies and then propose new measures. True, this is probably more difficult to manage in large complex, industrial societies like Britain—far more difficult than in Norway, for example, where Thomas Mathiesen has annually organized strategic "retreats" where sympathetic politicians, criminal justice administrators, and prisoners too, come together to discuss new initiatives. The process is therefore one of renewal. It is also one of vigilance; there is the need for members of the moral community to intervene where they can to defend its position from incursions from the *inner* and *outer* spheres.

What interests me about this framework is perhaps obvious. It is another way of describing how penal policy has been traditionally made in Britain. Of course, the fit is not exact. Prisoners have rarely been invited to join the moral community in Britain, and I doubt if many of the British moral community, including its academics, shared the genuinely radical, leftwing political aspirations of Thomas Mathiesen, or the connections he tried to establish between prisoners and the outside working classes. (He was keen to share these aspirations with members of Radical Alternatives to Prison, like myself, in the 1970s.) But leaving these differences aside, there is a lot of empirical evidence, as my own work over the years has shown, to support the view that a small, unrepresentative community of reformers, fearing the "uneducated" public voice and "unenlightened" operatives, has sought to shape the direction of penal policy making. We know that the format that this community has taken has changed over time, that its agenda has not always succeeded. But that is not the issue here. More to the point is how can it be justified in a modern democratic society?

On the face of it, Thomas Mathiesen at least has a very egalitarian thrust to his thinking. Doing business like this, keeping ordinary people at bay, patronizing them almost, somehow seems out of character. The answer, of course, is complicated. To start with, Mathiesen *does* engage with the public voice; he has been a great public campaigner and publicist. However, he increasingly despairs of being able to engage in rational public debate. Following Habermas (1989) on the decline of *communicative rationality* he wrote:

> Communicative rationality implies an emphasis on truthfulness, relevance and sincerity in argumentation. It was, in other words, possible to argue in a truthful manner with relevance and sincerity, and such argumentation was given at least some hearing, at the decision making level. The best example of this is the fall of the treatment philosophy. The fall occurred at least partly as a consequence of research into the effects of treatment, and it followed a relatively informed debate where the research results were an important part of the argument ... Today... communicative rationality lives its life in the secluded corners of the professional journals and meetings, while the public debate, flooded as it is by dire warnings by the police and sensational crime stories, and significantly, by opportunistic political initiatives in the context of burlesque television shows called "debates" is predominately characterized by the rationality of the market place.
>
> (Mathiesen 1995, p 8)

The media plays a pivotal role in denying communicative rationality; at a popular level the public is fed with simple solutions to complex problems, in our case penal problems.

These academic fears mirror liberal fears. Inviting in the public is a recipe for disaster. The media simplifies—even brutalizes—these complex issues. It is therefore best to deal with them more discreetly, away from the glare of publicity.

The press response to monitoring released paedophiles illustrates just how easily public opinion is inflamed. Even if Straw had been trying to engage in a rational dialogue over this difficult issue, and I think there is only a weak case to suggest that he was, and this he conducted through junior ministers from the safety of his Home Office bunker, he would have been blown off course by the Murdoch tabloids. No wonder then, he dived for cover, leaving it to others, particularly and significantly, the National Society for the Prevention of Cruelty to Children (NSPCC), to force a more informed debate. Of course, politicians must take some responsibility for the overall decline in the power of communicative rationality in public life, but that is another matter. As things stand, it is easy to see why the moral community in Britain looks *inwards* to engage with rational, though not always sympathetic, political and administrative elites, rather than looking *outwards* to an "inflammatory" public.

THE PUBLIC VOICE

I am not much interested here in asking whether or not this desire of the "moral community" to influence the direction of penal policy behind closed doors is arrogant, whether in Britain, at least, it represents little more, in truth, than a snobbish, liberal, educated, professional disdain for the views of ordinary folk in these matters. I am, however, interested in asking whether or not such a moral community can sustain its influence in our changing democracy. What I mean by this is that the hierarchical society I outlined in my first essay on the 1940s and 1950s, battered by the radicalism of the 1960s and 1970s and then further undermined by the consumerism of the 1980s and 1990s which transformed the criminal justice system into a service to be measured and consumed, has irrevocably changed.

People are less and less prepared to leave questions, including difficult penal questions, to their "masters". Nor are they, in less ideologically inclined times where less than a third of the electorate can see much difference between the parties, willing to leave such questions to "their" party which they are increasingly less inclined slavishly to vote for, that is even if they bother to vote at all. In short, to argue for what Mill described as the value of "superior wisdom" of elites, be it of politicians, pressure groups, university professors like Andrew Rutherford or other experts, nowadays cuts far less ice in a political culture which is moving away from deference, trusting instead to exerting more direct pressure through mechanisms outside of the formal political process and its network of consultative committees and processes.

This growing public "independence" is evident across a number of modern democracies, it is a post-modern phenomenon that has been extensively researched. Robert Inglehart, for example, writes:

> Mass publics have played a role in national politics for long time of course, through the ballot and in other ways. Current changes enable them to play an increasingly active role in formulating policy, and to engage in what might be called "elite-challenging", as opposed to "elite-directed" activities. Elite-directed participation is

largely a matter of elites mobilizing mass support through established organizations such as political parties, labour unions, religious institutions, and so on. The newer elite-challenging style of politics gives the public an increasingly important role in making specific *decisions*, not just a [mere] choice between two or more sets of decision makers.

(Inglehart, p 3)

Two processes are driving this long term change:

One aspect of the change in values, we believe, is a decline in the legitimacy of hierarchical authority, patriotism, religion and so on, which leads to declining confidence in institutions. At the same time, the political expression of new values is facilitated by a shift in the balance of political skills between elite and mass. Certain basic [political] skills seem to be changing in a gradual but deeply rooted fashion.

(Inglehart, p 4)

The political skills in question are a result of increased mass education and the growth of the information society through new technologies. These changes enable the masses to participate more in politics, they help ordinary people to acquire the skills (and information) previously enjoyed only by those within the formal political and administrative networks. One result of this is that:

Today *ad hoc* organizations can be brought into being more or less at will because the public has an unprecedentedly large leavening of non-elites possessing high levels of political skills. A balance between elites and mass that was upset centuries ago has been partially redressed.

(Inglehart, p 302)

Thus:

Western publics are developing an increasing potential for political participation. This change does not imply that mass publics will simply show higher rates of participation in traditional activities such as voting, but that they may intervene in the political process on a qualitatively different level. Increasingly they are likely to demand participation in making major decisions, not just a voice in selecting the decision makers ... These changes have important implications for political parties, labour unions and professional organizations; for mass politics are increasingly likely to be elite-challenging rather than elite-directed.

(Inglehart, p 294)

Overall then, he believes that: "there has been a shift between elites and mass; and as a result, even lower status groups may be increasing their ability to make significant political inputs" (Inglehart, p 297).

While it is important to remember that Ingelehart's research crossed several continents, and that Britain, for all the decline in deference, is still more deferential than Ronald Inglehart's America, what he is saying has a clear resonance for Britain. Here parties have become far more responsive to changing public sentiment on specific issues as opposed to offering broad, ideologically distinctive programmes to the electorate once every four or five years. In its turn, the electorate has shown less and less inclination to turn out to vote, even at

General Elections, believing that it does not matter that much which party is in power. This has led Peter Riddle to observe the paradox that with the collapse of Communism liberal democracies like our own have never been stronger, yet formal political institutions and processes count for less, particularly among the young, and are used less then they ever were (*The Times*, 19 June 2000).

The force of these changes in our political culture was brought home to Britain in the summer of 2000. During August of that year a few lorries began picketing an oil refinery just outside of Manchester. This was in protest against fuel costs that had steadily risen, partly because of price rises on the international market, and partly through the application of the fuel tax "escalator" first introduced by a previous Conservative government. Within a day or so the picketing lorry drivers were joined by other disaffected groups, including small dairy farmers with their tractors. Quickly Britain's fuel supplies were almost cut off and the government lurched into a full-scale political crisis with opinion polls showing overwhelming support for the protesters who, through their skilful use of digital mobile telephone and fax networks, seemed to have the country at their mercy (Rawnsley 2001, *Chapter 20*). It is no exaggeration to say that the government seemed to be as close to being toppled then as it had been during any of its previous struggles against organized labour going back the General Strike of 1926.

When this loose alliance eventually broke up after the government signalled that it would make some concessions in the forthcoming budget, particularly to the road haulage industry, the long term damage to the New Labour government was not serious: the protest was not an ideologically based protest in the traditional sense of being an old-fashioned party struggle between capital and labour, rather it was a "consumers' protest". Within a year New Labour was returned with another huge majority, but significantly it was the lowest turnout at any General Election since 1918.

It is, of course, easy to berate the simplicity of the arguments of many of those who took part in this protest. Like the people of Paulsgrove, they wanted simple populist solutions to what are, in truth, complex policy problems. However, the crucial point is that the protest reveals how easily the public voice can be translated into effective political action quite outside of the parties, or indeed, any of the other traditional institutions that channel communication between people and government in modern democratic societies. Furthermore, although New Labour miscalculated on this issue, as it arguably mishandled the Paulsgrove episode, both protests are testimony to the claim that there is:

> An upgrading of the public voice in political communication. Instead of being positioned only to attend to and overhear the views and arguments of others (politicians, journalists, pressure group spokesmen) the experience and opinions of quite ordinary people are being aired more often.

> (Blumler and Gurevitch 1996, p 129).

This upgrading of the public voice is partly a consequence of the growth in commercial media outlets from the late 1950s onwards, and new media technologies. The days have long since gone when the only voice governments had to listen to on controversial issues like capital punishment was Lord Reith's respectful BBC. The introduction of commercial television—this was akin to introducing the bubonic plague into Britain according to Lord Reith in 1957 (Sampson 1962)—began upgrading the public voice, and the truth of the matter is that with the recent arrival of digital networks there are so many outlets that any old "riff raff" are invited on air to give their views on such subjects, indeed, some even do some agenda setting of their own. Or if you cannot get air space to talk about what concerns you, why not email the Prime Minister's Office, or log on to the Downing Street web page?[3]

These wider, political and cultural changes which have upgraded the public voice have been reinforced by significant changes within the criminal justice system itself. That is to say, it seems fairly obvious to me that the repositioning of the public voice is partly a reflection of the simple fact that governments now need to engage with the public in a way that was not envisaged in the decades immediately after 1945. At this time the machinery of law and order, as we have seen, was firmly in the hands of a highly centralized State and the security of each and every one of us was entrusted to, and jealously guarded by, those who operated the formal levers of law and order. This began to change in the 1980s when it became apparent that the central State could no longer deliver on law and order from the centre and the result has been the restructuring of the delivery of these services, including penal services, to engage the public. Sometimes it engages them in a voluntary rather than a paid capacity, sometimes they participate at local level rather than national level.

The result is that as individuals and as groups, often in partnership with professionals from both the private and public sectors, citizens are being invited back into the criminal justice network. For Garland this marks

> what may be the beginning of an important reconfiguration of the "criminal justice state" and its relation to the citizen. Other developments—such as the rise of the victims' movement and the enhanced role accorded to victims in the criminal and sentencing process, or the development of reparation and mediation schemes on the fringes of the system—reinforce this view.
>
> (Garland 1996)

The involvement of the "active citizen" in England and Wales leading to the "re-invention" of governance in this important aspect of our daily lives has been traced by others (Benyon and Edwards 2001).

This increasing public stake has enhanced the public voice. Governments cannot mobilize active citizens and then ignore them. A dialogue, sometimes it can be both crude and ill informed, is now increasingly demanded. The public refuses to be air brushed out of the penal equation, it is now more embedded in the architecture of the policy making process. This development is as much an integral part of post-modern penality, as some academics like to call it, as the current emphasis on containment at the expense of rehabilitation (Hallsworth 2002). It is also, in my view, a development that has to be understood and located outside the formal sociology of moral panics.

---

[3] The potential of communicating online is well understood by New Labour which has a Cabinet sub-committee on E-democracy (*The Times, 29 April 2002*).

What I mean by this is that we have seen since 1945 several occasions when political parties deliberately helped to generate, or at the very least, sustain moral panics for their own, wider political purposes, tapping into public fears about crime and punishment and producing a punitive backlash. I think the Conservatives did this without the slightest compunction in the 1970s and New Labour, though to a far lesser extent, did so around the murder of James Bulger in the 1990s. There will always be such panics, and postgraduate sociology students will doubtless continue to do good work trying to trace their course. The better students will then make judgements about the political costs and benefits involved in these moments, to explore their wider political purposes, which may turn out to have little to do with penality *per se*.

But the truth of the matter is such panics come and go, and the public's fear or anger over this or that law and order issue eventually fades, though in suggesting this I would not dispute that in recent decades the public mood has become increasingly insecure and punitive in the face of rising crime rates (Garland 2001). However, the development I have been tracing in this essay points to *something else at work,* namely, that for a quite different set of reasons our democracy is changing, and that the transmission of public preferences into the heart of government, demanding day by day that more attention be given to them, is something that all politicians increasingly have to learn to live with, and this most certainly includes home secretaries (Ryan 1999).

Consequences

I now want to ask whether or not this upsurge in the public voice, and the necessity for politicians to heed it, is a good or bad thing, and what this might mean for those penal lobby groups who in the public mind represent what Jack Straw figuratively (and pejoratively) refers to as Hampstead liberals, or what has elsewhere been identified as constituting the "moral community."

Some readers, perhaps with my account of Paulsgrove fresh in their minds, will feel some unease that I even need to consider such a question. I well understand this unease. According to one strand of democratic theory the prospect of paying more attention to the public voice is certainly not at all promising. Indeed, *the consequential downgrading of intermediate groups* is seen as a recipe for authoritarian rather than democratic government because it fails to acknowledge that democracy is less about government by the people, but more a set of complicated institutional arrangements whereby the various publics in any society, including what we have referred as public opinion more broadly defined, work out compromises which are, by and large, accepted by all the parties, including the broader public.

If this complicated, often infuriating, always aggravating, process is bypassed then the voters, left isolated and without any form of counter intelligence, fall easy prey to manipulation by political leaders through devices like focus groups or opinion polls.

According to this strand of democratic theory, Stanley Greenberg's observation, accepted as fact by Philip Gould, that the "institutions that used to be effective in mediating popular sentiment have atrophied and have lost their ability to articulate ... If you want to know what ... people think ... polls and focus groups are the best available means" is deeply worrying (quoted by Gould

1998, p 333). Political parties, trade unions and so on, apparently no longer represent anything or anyone much.

The logic of this view is that even if we believe, as Philip Gould apparently believes, that British governments are altogether more benign than this suggests, that *all* they *genuinely* want to know is what it is the public really wants, then boldly phrased democratic politics is no longer about governments carrying out programmes they have sold to the public. Instead, it is more about finding out what people want and then doing it. "Consumer politics", untainted by groups which either do not express the public's views, or seek to undermine them, should take the place of "producer politics" (Gould 1998). You do not tell the electorate that selling council houses is a bad thing. If people want to buy council houses then let them do it. If people believe that longer sentences can defeat crime then let them have longer sentences, forget that the Howard League, INQUEST or the Prison Reform Trust tell you they will not work. Who, after all, do these groups represent? They represent nobody but themselves, a motley crew of Hampstead liberals, radical academics and a few do-gooding magistrates and their clerks who try to persuade governments that their "expert" views should take precedence over everyone else's as "they know best". For Gould, allowing the broader public to have their say is not manipulation, but representation.

When pressed, Gould subsequently articulated a somewhat different picture in an exchange with Ian Aitken (*The Guardian*, 24, 26 and 28 August 1999). His thesis, he says, is not as I and others represent it, rather he accepts that politics is fundamentally about holding to values and principles. This, in fairness to Gould, implicitly accepts that governments still need to make judgements, and that sometimes these judgements will involve compromising with public opinion in the light of what other groups, institutions or experts advise. So, in the two examples I have just cited, experts might warn that selling too many council houses could seriously damage the efficiency of public services if key workers are unable to find accommodation in inner cities; that in the case of higher sentences for paedophiles, the penal lobby may suggest that this will only have only a very marginal effect in tackling what is a serious problem.

So in these cases a lot of information, opinions will be laid on the table. Gould's refined position appears to be that in taking such information on board, perhaps making compromises, the broader public has the right to have its views known and represented—and that *very often in the past this has not been the case.* Too often difficult issues have been quietly settled, not least in matters of crime and punishment, between government and the *cognoscenti* with consumers of such services, battered women for example, being left out in the cold. His work is about putting the consumers' views in the frame, of acknowledging that in today's society the public voice can no longer be ignored.

I find this refinement far more palatable, not least because as Margaret Canovan wisely reminds us, we should never lose sight of the redemptive promise of democracy. Democracy should never *just* be articulated as a complicated way of reaching decisions, its promise is that the manner in which decisions are settled confers some power and authority on those who participate, including the broader public, *that is what underpins its legitimacy* (Canovan 1999). There is not much mileage in trying to mobilize the people around the idea that democracy is *just* a series of checks and balances, that democratic politics is little more than a series of messy compromises arrived at behind closed doors among the *cognoscenti*. Of course, selling the redemptive version of democracy by suggesting at heady moments that "the people are the masters now" runs the risk of stoking up populist expectations, but as Canovan argues, it is not unreasonable to interpret populism as the necessary "shadow of democracy". (For a participative approach, see Johnstone 2001.)

Of course, this essay is testimony to the obvious truth that Gould's analysis is far less concerned than it should be with how the broader public voice he seeks to both measure and articulate is *socially constructed*, and that it fails to question seriously what wider political purposes the voice might serve, particularly at moments of acute social tension. In this sense, Gould's apparent psephological sophistication seems to be accompanied by sociological naiveté or political instrumentalism, or both. (But then, the same may also apply to Lord Windlesham.) Furthermore, when it suits his purpose, Gould shares with many of us a tendency to slip into the habit of speaking of the broader public voice as being a far more homogenous construct than it really is, as if translating this voice as a form of legitimacy is without serious problems (Ruggiero 1991). Nonetheless, his argument that governments increasingly have to attend to the public voice(s), and that this may be no bad thing for democracy, surely has some validity, even if it threatens to make the always difficult business of government even more trying than it was in the 1940s and 1950s.

A FOOTNOTE TO RALLY THE HAMPSTEAD LIBERALS

Even though New Labour's repressive, social authoritarianism hardly sits comfortably with their principles of tolerance, Hampstead liberals and the groups they represent can at least take a little comfort from where we are now. After all, the traditional penal lobby has been repositioned but not entirely ignored, and in spite of its rhetoric, New Labour once in office has slowly come to realize that knowledge, considered judgement, expertise, such qualities matter, that good government is about more than just reading printouts of simple public opinion polls or focus groups. This is reassuring to a degree. However, the growing importance of the public voice will not go away. Traditional lobby groups no longer have governments all to themselves.

Of course, this is not a sudden change, nor is it simply the result of more populist times. I pointed out in my third essay, for example, that "efficiency" experts now have the inside track and that changes in the nature of governance have fractured and transformed central government, making policy networks far more diffuse, crowded and more difficult to influence than they once were (Ryan, Savage and Wall 2001). These changes have been taking place for some time. So the contrast is not between today and the narrow, cosy world I outlined in my first essay.

As I have argued, however, central government and its agencies are still the source of much policy making and still oversee policy implementation, so the lobby still needs to work these new networks, and indeed, is still surprisingly successful at this. Its discreet game of musical chairs goes on. For example, over the last few years the director of the Prison Reform Trust, Stephen Shaw, has turned up as the Prisons and Probation Ombudsman; David Faulkner, formerly at the Home Office, now teaches criminology at Oxford and was for a time the Chair of the Howard League; some leading Home Office researchers, Mike Hough, for example, now occupy university posts; Professor Rod Morgan, an academic member of Faulkner's liberal *ensemble* is now the Chief Inspector of the Probation Service; Ann Owers who ran Justice so successfully for many years is now Her Majesty's Chief Inspector of Prisons. And as he might describe himself as a "liberal" of sorts in this context, we should not forget that Douglas Hurd left office and became the Chairman of the Prison Reform Trust. The boundary between government and outside bodies seems to be rapidly blurring.

Of course, that these interlocking networks, sucking as they do more and more people into governance, carry the potential to limit effective, principled opposition and to stifle genuine creative thinking is perhaps obvious, and those enjoying the fruits of these new networks, including academics like myself, might well reflect on this. However, the real danger of this continuing insider strength is that this is exactly what it is, it looks *inwards* rather than *outwards*, rarely moving beyond the increasingly diffuse machinery of central government at a time when the political parties are being forced more and more to engage with the public voice.

This may have worked in the past, when nobody took much notice of the consumers of criminal justice services. But what this liberal lobby needs to do now is to engage with the wider public more, and with central government less. Without this, the redemptive promise of democracy, which carries with it—even in Mill, for example—the requirement (and *promise*) of political education, will degenerate even more frequently than it does now into penal populism. That the liberal lobby has failed to do just that, it has had "little impact in terms of restraining the development of penal populism", is the harsh criticism that has recently been made of it by people who are probably more closely identified with its liberal sentiments than I am (Roberts *et al.* 2002). But not only does the liberal lobby need to engage more, it needs to engage *differently*, to improve and vary its styles of communication, and above all, to think more strategically about the sites on which it needs to engage populist sentiment.

Making the most of such opportunities is no easy business, nobody is suggesting that it is. We have in Britain, more than in most other European countries, a mostly right wing populist press, now assiduously cultivated by *both* the major political parties, that makes "communicative rationality" difficult (Downes 1991). Who would not rather look inwards than confront marauding parents using children who can barely walk in their ill-informed crusade against paedophiles named and shamed by *The News of the World*? Who does not despair when another cynical red top editor wheels out, nearly 40 years after the event, the still grieving mother of Lesley Anne Downey whose daughter was so brutally murdered by Myra Hindley and Ian Brady? Add to this malign press influence a political culture which, since the mobilization of the Bloody Code in the eighteenth century, has secured wider political change around the rhetoric and symbols of law and order and the difficulties of engaging in a constructive dialogue with the public becomes readily apparent.

However, Golding (1995) has done well to remind us that there are other more optimistic views about the possibility of a "communicative rationality" around the emergence of the new technologies and new social movements which suggest a more vibrant, progressive, less purely nationally focussed, homogeneous "public voice(s)" than we sometimes suppose. So there is some hope for Thomas Mathiesen's "alternative" public forum (Mathiesen 1995, pp 8–9). If people, often young and poorly resourced people, can organize across national boundaries and mobilize against world trade negotiators using the new technologies I fail to see why others cannot do the same on narrower terrain. Indeed, there are already a number of quite sophisticated "alternative" web-sites on penal questions, including capital punishment (Roberts *et al.* 2002). This encouragement, however, does comes with the warning that this "alternative" public can all too easily degenerate into a small group of activists talking to themselves; radicals can detach themselves from the public just as easily as metropolitan elites, as my second essay testifies. (To put the same thing another way, a brief Internet search will turn up a variety of inchoate, populist sites, and engagement with these is arguably more important than talking to the converted.)

So, the liberal penal lobby needs to engage more. Without reaching out, say through the Howard League's commendable if limited initiative on citizenship and crime, or making more of Mike Hough's research which shows that if properly informed the *public voice(s)* is not as crude as the tabloids represent it, the lobby will be left simply reacting to punitive populist responses (Hough and Roberts 1998). Of course, conventional lobbying will continue to be needed, defensive initiatives will also be required from time to time, and some credit should be given the NSPCC, NACRO, the chief police officers involved in ACPO and the chief officers of probation (ACOP) who took on *The News of the World* over its crude campaign to "unmask" paedophiles while politicians mostly stayed in their bunkers (*The News of the World*, 6 August 2000). However, in late modernity where the power of the public voice(s) is growing, a far more proactive approach is needed and a successful strategy needs to involve more than just making sure that the "usual" people turn up in the "right" places.

The truth of the matter is that Hampstead liberals, or those who do not bridle too much at such a label, have mostly been slotted into what were once the "right" places. The problem is that they are less effectual than they once were, and while they have continued earnestly to organize among themselves to secure a less repressive penal system for disciplining the working classes—and more power to their elbow for trying to make use of their privileged backgrounds in this way against New Labour—the prison population has soared, conditions for release on parole and licence have become more restrictive and, partly as a consequence of technology, the overall penal apparatus has arguably become more intrusive than it ever was. Moreover, one reading of the government's recent review of sentencing policy (Home Office 2001) suggests that things might even get worse (*The Guardian*, 29 January 2002). Already the prison population is predicted to reach 70,000. by the summer of 2002. So there is a lot of ground to be recovered. Hampstead liberals might try representing themselves to the public instead of leaving politicians like Jack Straw or David Blunkett to do it for them, even if it weakens the patronage that has traditionally secured their access to government. Indeed, that might be the best place to start.

REFERENCES for *Part IV*

Anderson P. and Mann N. (1997) *Safety First: the Making of New Labour* (London: Grant)

Benyon J. and Edwards A. (2001) "Networking and Crime Control at Local Level" in Ryan M., Savage S. and Wall D. (eds.) *Policy Networks in Criminal Justice* (London: Palgrave)

Bloomer J. and Gurevitch M. (1966) "Mass Media and Society" in Curran J. and Gurevitch M. (eds.) *Media Change and Social Change* (London: Arnold)

Bottoms A. (1995) "The Politics and Philosophy of Sentencing" in Clarkson C. and Morgan R. (eds.) *The Politics of Sentencing Reform* (Oxford: Clarendon), pp 17-49

Canovan M. (1999) "Trust the People! Populism and the Two Faces of Democracy" *Political Studies* XLV11, pp 2–16

Conservative Party *Manifesto 1979* (London: Conservative Party)

Corrigan P., Jones T., Lloyd J. and Young J. (1988) *Socialism, Merit and Efficiency* (London: Fabian Society, No. 530)

Downes D. (1991) "The Origins and Consequences of Dutch Penal Policy since 1945" in Muncie J. and Sparks R. (eds.) *Imprisonment: European Perspectives* (London: Harvester)

Dunbar I. and Langdon A. (1998) *Tough Justice* (London: Blackstone)

Garland D. (1996) "The Limits of the Sovereign State: Strategies of Crime Control in Contemporary Society" *British Journal of Criminology*, vol. 30, pp 449–474

Garland D. (2000) *The Culture of Control* (Oxford: Oxford University Press)

Golding P. (1995) "The Mass Media and the Public Sphere: The Crisis of Information in the 'Information Society'" in Edgell S., Walklate S. and Williams G. (eds.) *Debating the Future of the Public Sphere* (Aldershot: Avebury)

Gould P. (1998) *The Unfinished Revolution* (London: Little Brown)

Habermas J. (1989) *The Structural Transformation of the Public Sphere: An Inquiry Into a Category of Bourgeois Society* (Massachusetts: MIT Press)

Hall S. *et al.* (1978) *Policing the Crisis* (London: Macmillan)

Hall S. (1979) "The Great Moving Right Show" *Marxism Today*, 23 (1) January

Hallsworth S. (2002) "The Case for a Postmodern Penality: Reconsidered and Reaffirmed" *Theoretical Criminology*, vol. 6 (2), pp145–163

Home Office (2001) *Making Punishments Work: Report of a Review of the Sentencing Framework for England and Wales* (London: HMSO)

Hough M. and Roberts J. (1998) *Attitudes to Punishment: Findings from the British Crime Survey*. Home Office Research Study 179 (London: Home Office)

Inglehart R. (1997) *The Silent Revolution* (Princeton: Princeton University Press)

Johnstone G. (2001) "Penal Policy Making: Elitist, Populist or Participatory?" *Punishment and Society*, vol. 2 (2), pp 161—180

Jonker J. (1986) *Victims of Violence* (London: Fontana)

Kinsey R., Lea J. and Young J. (1986) *Losing the Fight Against Crime* (Oxford: Blackwell)

Mathiesen T. (1995) *Driving Forces Behind Prison Growth: the Mass Media* (International Conference on Prison Growth, Oslo, Norway)

Melossi D. (1994) "The 'Economy' of Illegalities: Normal Crimes, Elites and Social Control" in Nelken D. (ed.) *Comparative Analysis in the Futures of Criminology* (Sage: London), pp 202–219

Newburn T. (1995) *Crime and Criminal Justice Policy* (London: Longman)

Rentoul J. (1995) *Tony Blair* (London: Little, Brown and Co)

Roberts J., Stalans L., Indermaur D. and Hough M. (2002) *Penal Populism and Public Opinion* (Oxford: Oxford University Press)

Rock P. (1990) *Helping Victims of Crime* (Oxford: Clarendon Press)

Rock P. (1998) *After Homicide* (Oxford: Clarendon Press)

Rogaly J. (1977) *Grunwick* (Harmondsworth: Penguin)

Ruggiero V. (1991) "Public Opinion and Penal Reform in Britain" *Crime, Law and Social Change*, vol. 15, pp 37–50

Rutherford A. (1995) *Transforming Criminal Policy: Spheres of Influence in the United States, The Netherlands and England and Wales during the 1980s* (Winchester: Waterside Press)

Ryan M. (1983) *The Politics of Penal Reform* (London: Longman)

Ryan M. (1999) "Penal Policy Making Toward the Millennium: Elites and Populists. New Labour and the New Criminology" *International Journal of the Sociology of Law* vol. 27, pp 1–22

Ryan M., Savage S. and Wall D. (eds.) (2001) *Policy Networks in Criminal Justice* (London: Palgrave)

Scraton P. (1987) *Law, Order and the Authoritarian State* (Milton Keynes: Open University Press)

Sim J. (2000) "Against the Punitive Wind: Stuart Hall, the State and the Lessons of the Great Moving Right Show" in Gilroy P., Grossberg L. and McRobbie A. (eds.) *Without Guarantees* (London: Verso)

Sparks R. (1996) *Penal Politics and Politics Proper: New "Austerity" and Contemporary English Political Culture.* (Law and Society Association Conference, University of Strathclyde)

Swaaningen R. van and Jonge G. de (1995) "The Dutch Prison System and Penal Policy in the 1990s: From Humanitarian Paternalism to Penal Business Management" in Ruggiero V., Ryan M. and Sim J. (eds.) (1995) *Western European Penal Systems: A Critical Anatomy* (London: Sage)

Taylor I. (1981) *Law and Order Arguments for Socialism* (London: Macmillan)

Windlesham, Lord (1993) *Response to Crime* (Oxford: Clarendon)

Young J. and Lea J. (1984) *What is to be Done about Law and Order?* (Harmondsworth: Penguin)

Index

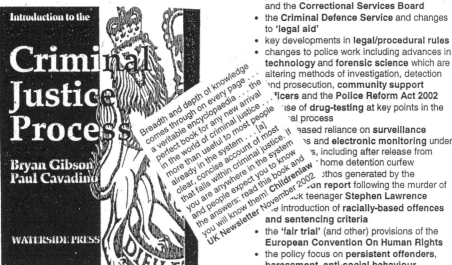

As featured in *The Times* and *Daily Telegraph*

Crime, State and Citizen
A FIELD FULL OF FOLK

David Faulkner

A wide-ranging and authoritative appraisal of the factors which sustain the fragile balance between effective government and individual rights and obligations in modern-day Britain. It is about: how Britain governs itself today; the rights and responsibilities of its citizens; the character of its public services and their relations with the state. **With a Foreword by Lord Windlesham.**

Highly recommended . . . This is an extraordinary book and could not have been published at a better time: *Criminal Practitioners Newsletter*

A masterly analysis of the relationships between state and people . . . Throughout this excellent volume our beliefs and prejudices about crime are tried and tested: *The Justices' Clerk*

This is simply the best book I have ever read on criminal justice; it is quite possibly the best one ever written. It is wide-ranging, comprehensive, detailed, analytical and authoritative. It is also bang up to date . . . It is a book that should be read and kept by anyone and everyone who has a finger in the criminal justice pie. It will be a long time before it is excelled: *Justice of the Peace*

Faulkner has done a great service by reminding us that investment in new legislation, management systems and technology will be of small worth unless civic values of society are reflected in such developments: *Scolag Legal Journal*

Writing at a time when issues such as the Rule of Law, human rights and cultural and human diversity are to the fore, David Faulkner examines these and similar issues by focusing on the politics and policies, and the professional standards and day-to-day arrangements, for dealing with crime and criminal justice in England and Wales - touching on matters of immediate concern to Parliament, the Government, the courts, the criminal justice services and individuals. He also explores the underlying aims and principles of justice, social inclusion, public safety (including matters of concern to victims of crime), accountability and legitimacy before suggesting how they should be applied and conflicts resolved. **ISBN 1 872 870 98 8. £22.50 plus £2.50 p&p**

Available from Waterside Press at the address overleaf.